Play Therapy and
Asperger's Syndrome

Play Therapy and Asperger's Syndrome

Helping Children and Adolescents Grow, Connect, and Heal through the Art of Play

Kevin B. Hull, Ph.D.

JASON ARONSON
Lanham • Boulder • New York • Toronto • Plymouth, UK

Published by Jason Aronson
A wholly owned subsidary of Rowman & Littlefield
4501 Forbes Boulevard, Suite 200, Lanham, Maryland 20706
www.rowman.com

10 Thornbury Road, Plymouth PL6 7PP, United Kingdom

British Library Cataloguing in Publication Information Available

Library of Congress Cataloging-in-Publication Data
The hardback edition of this book was previously cataloged by the Library of Congress as
follows:

Hull, Kevin B., 1971–
  Play therapy and Asperger's syndrome : helping children and adolescents grow,
connect, and heal through the art of play / Kevin B. Hull.
    p. cm.
  Includes bibliographical references and index.
  I. Title.
  [DNLM: 1. Asperger Syndrome—therapy. 2. Asperger Syndrome—diagnosis.
3. Play Therapy—methods. WS 350.8.P4]
  LC classification not assigned
  HV4005.I45 2011
  618.92'858832—dc23
                                    2011030442

ISBN 978-0-7657-0856-4 (cloth : alk. paper)
ISBN 978-0-7657-1019-2 (pbk. : alk. paper)
ISBN 978-0-7657-0857-1 (electronic)

Printed in the United States of America

This book is dedicated to the many children, adolescents, and adults diagnosed with Asperger's syndrome and their families who have invited me into their world and allowed me to see a place full of wonder and miracles.

In Loving Memory of my mother, Nancy Anne Hull, who was the first person to show me the wonder and beauty of play.

Contents

Acknowledgments   ix

Preface   xi

Chapter 1   In His Own Little World—Living with
                 Asperger's Syndrome   1

Chapter 2   What Is Asperger's Syndrome?   7

Chapter 3   Potential Challenges of Therapy with Children and
                 Adolescents Diagnosed with Asperger's Syndrome   13

Chapter 4   The Therapeutic Alliance, Empathy, and Themes in
                 Play Therapy with Children Diagnosed with
                 Asperger's Syndrome   21

Chapter 5   Play Therapy Toys and Techniques with Children
                 Diagnosed with Asperger's Syndrome   31

Chapter 6   Creating Connection and Examination of Themes in
                 Play Therapy with Adolescents Diagnosed with
                 Asperger's Syndrome   55

Chapter 7   Play Therapy with Adolescents Diagnosed with
                 Asperger's Syndrome   79

Chapter 8   Divorce and Grief and Loss Issues   113

Epilogue   143

Johnny's Letter   145

Bibliography   149

Index   155

About the Author   161

Acknowledgments

I first want to acknowledge all my teachers, professors, and mentors that I have had over the years who instilled a love of learning in me and who taught me the value of seeking knowledge. And to my friends who never stopped believing in me and who sometimes carried me through the valleys of life; you know who you are. To my lovely wife and children, you have brought me great healing and joy and inspiration, and you renew my spirit each day to go and help others; I could never put into words the strength you give me. To my parents, who modeled for me the power of putting the needs of others first and showed me that the servants really do inherit the earth, I thank you. To my brothers and their families, who gave me a great deal of encouragement during this endeavor, I thank you also.

To Dr. Ronald Allen, who taught me the power of imagination in the play therapy process with children and adolescents; to Dr. John Thomas, who gave me endless encouragement and guidance in my graduate training and taught me how to write; to Dr. Michael Sligh, who encouraged me as a friend, professional, and spiritual mentor; to Dr. David Crenshaw, who graciously responded to my e-mails which set this whole writing thing in motion in the first place and whose books have provided so much knowledge for my work; to Dr. Byron Norton, who through passionately presenting his work at a conference in Tampa in 1997 lit a fire in me to pursue learning as much as I could about play therapy; to those who serve with me and teach others: Frank, Jana, Adam, Rick, Treena, Rhett, Norma, and Kim; to my students, who through listening to lectures have helped me put what I do into words; to the "giants" of the field, too numerous to name, who have labored and served to make play therapy a force in helping young people; and finally, to the individuals who have labored so intensely in the world of autism and Asperger's syndrome: Simon Baron-Cohen, Dan LeGoff, Tony Attwood, John Greally, Richard Bromfield, and countless others, to you I offer my sincere gratefulness for helping people like me get to do what I do.

Finally, my sincere thanks to Samantha Kirk for her editing expertise and guidance during this process; and to all the staff at Jason Aronson who helped bring this work into book form, I thank you.

Preface

I love to play. I have been playing since, well, for a long time. By the time I was three or four, I was playing out whole football games all by myself. Donned in my Pittsburgh Steelers number 58 Jack Lambert jersey and my football helmet, I would be the quarterback, wide receiver, running back, and the defensive players. I would throw myself down on the ground rolling in the mud, believing I had been tackled by a huge lineman. I imagined my coach calling timeout and I would sit on my helmet just like the real players did. After a short break, back in I would go and run and throw and score the winning touchdown just as the clock expired. I would limp to the sidelines like my heroes did on the TV, dirty, tired, and inexplicably joyous. I had no idea my parents and two older brothers were watching the whole thing from the kitchen window laughing at my imaginary world, which to me, was as real as what I saw on TV.

School was a cruel shock to me because playtime was limited. I continued to play long after the teacher had instructed us not to, and this led to problems. I repeated third grade because of this and could not understand why we had to be inside when it was so nice outside. I imagined bars on all the windows, the classrooms felt like the below-decks of a ship, I would literally shake as we lined up for recess finally about to be released from the stifling environment. I could not get enough of play. My imagination was huge, and I could not explain the joy that I felt creating imaginary worlds complete with civilizations, armies, and wild creatures. I never lost my love of play even into my teens and early adult years, and when I took a job at the Florida Baptist Children's Home in Lakeland, Florida, I realized that my love of play was a valuable tool in connecting with children and adolescents.

While working for a community mental health center in 1997, I attended a week long play therapy conference in Tampa taught by Dr. Byron Norton, who passionately shared his work and I rejoiced to find that my love of play could be used to help children and adolescents in therapy. The rest, as they say, is history. In 2001, I received my first referral of a young man formally diagnosed with Asperger's syndrome and I began to research every article and book I could get my hands on about Asperger's and have not stopped. Today, I receive many referrals of children, adolescents, and adults diagnosed with Asperger's syndrome into my practice, and I conduct individual sessions as well as group sessions each week. I am passionate about working with this population and am amazed and honored each week to be exposed to the keen observations, hilarious stories, and touching accounts of personal challenges and struggles that these amazing young people allow me to share.

The stories that I have shared in this book are all true, but the identities and some of the background details have been changed for confidentiality purposes. I have thoughtfully and carefully provided techniques and scenarios for the student or clinician who is new to the process of play therapy and the world of Asperger's syndrome, but I have also been mindful of the seasoned professional seeking to refine their skills. I have focused on providing you the reader a snapshot of techniques for skill building, but also have attempted to provide a solid foundation of the research that has been painstakingly done by so many brilliant and gifted people. Because of my training in family systems therapy, I have included sections for helping the families of these amazing young people; families comprised of parents/caregivers and siblings who are on the front lines daily and who become tired and fearful of the unknown. These parents and caregivers need us to help them learn skills in connecting with their young person and remind them how to play. Together, all of us create a powerful force in helping these remarkable young people connect, grow, and heal.

Chapter 1

In His Own Little World—Living with Asperger's Syndrome

THE CASE OF ROGER

Roger, an average-looking eight-year-old enters the hallway that leads toward the therapy room. He is accompanied by his mother. He is wide-eyed with an inquisitive look on his face. Just as he is about to enter the room, Roger stops and looks at the door frame, as if he is a building inspector. He glances at the top two corners and follows the frame to where the frame meets the floor, takes a deep breath, whispers something inaudible, and walks through. Once he is in the room, Roger stays close to his mother, who invites him to sit on the couch next to her. Roger methodically inspects the couch visually, running his eyes from one end to the other, and peeking down to make sure he can see where the legs of the couch touch the floor. Once he has completed his couch inspection, he sits. Roger has made no eye contact during his brief time in the therapy office, either with his mother or the therapist. Once sitting on the couch he keeps his eyes on the floor, glancing slightly to the left, and then to the right.

Gradually, Roger lifts his gaze and begins to look around the room. His eyes take in every detail of the room, and the tension in his face softens when his eyes light upon a box of Lego bricks in the corner. His mouth brightens slightly into a smile, Roger mouths something to himself, and then he settles back onto the couch nestled closely to his mother. The therapist speaks to Roger and for a brief instant Roger looks up at the therapist, and then quickly away. Roger does not respond to the therapist's questions. He only stares at the floor again. The therapist asks Roger if he would like to play with the Lego bricks. Roger does not respond; he only sits next to his mother.

While this is the first time that the therapist and Roger have met, it is the second meeting between the therapist and Roger's mother. In the first meeting, designed to provide a time for history taking and allowing Roger's mother to understand the approach of the therapist, Roger's mother shared about the sad, difficult, and sometimes humorous situations surrounding Roger's short eight years on the planet. She shared how he was, in her words, "In his own little world." She told of how Roger did not want to spend time with anyone but only immediate family that he knew very well. At school he had no friends; he simply watched when the other children played on the playground, as if they were a movie or a stage play, and he was a member of the audience. He liked being around others, but there was no interaction. He could share facts with others, mounds of information came out of him like he was an old-fashioned cash register spewing out reams of receipt tape, but there was no back-and-forth communication with peers.

Roger's mother shared about how he was "very smart"; in fact his IQ was shown to be at the very highest ranges. She told the therapist all the amazing facts he could recall and the things he could put together, and the things he had figured out on the computer. She also talked about Roger's fears and worries that went along with the high intelligence. Fears like germs, taking a bath, lightning, fire, masks, and throwing up—just to name a few. Some were not as severe as they were when Roger was younger; some had just popped up in the last few months. She also shared about the obsessions that Roger often exhibited. He could watch the same show or see the same clip on YouTube thousands of times in a row. He could sit at the computer or at a video game, or watch his favorite movie, for hours at a time. He then could talk about what he had seen without stopping for a few hours more. He did not seem to notice that others were tired of hearing it and ignored their comments as if he did not hear them. He was like a machine, almost robotic and seemingly unaware of the facial expressions or comments of others.

He wanted to eat the same foods at the same times on the same days and wear the same clothes. Despite his high intelligence, school was beginning to be difficult because of the rigidity that Roger displayed and his fears that seemed more intense with the daily school schedule. The school officials suspected that Roger possessed higher intelligence, yet he struggled with almost every assignment. Roger's mother told of the bullying that had begun. She said now that Roger was older he stood out more and more from the other children. Not that his behavior was new to the teachers or other students, but the odd behavior and lack of interaction with others was beginning to bring negative attention from his peers. Roger's mother shared how the school officials had recommended Roger should undergo testing by a local psychologist. "That's how I even found out about this, this Asperger-thing or whatever," she said. Roger's mother shared that she was considering home-schooling him, feeling that the home-schooling would make things easier for Roger and for her. "He seems like he needs some breathing space," she said, "Like he is very overwhelmed and by the time he comes home he is exhausted." "I'm exhausted," she sighed, looking down at the floor. "I feel like a failure," she said, with tears beginning to flow. "I'm just scared that I can't give him what he needs."

This current session was designed to bring the therapist and Roger together. The therapist got on the floor and moved closer to Roger, careful to not invade his space. He invited Roger to come over to some shelves where there were several toys for Roger to choose from. Roger glanced at the therapist, only for a second, and then began to whisper to himself. His mother told the therapist in their first meeting that whenever Roger was introduced to a new situation or person he would whisper to himself, as if he was gently reassuring himself or soothing himself. Roger's mother encouraged Roger to look at the toys, and slowly he began to inch closer to the shelves, glancing up ever so slightly. His eyes lighted upon a box of Lego bricks that stood out from the other toys, and he slowly reached up and took down the box. Then he opened it cautiously, whispering to himself. He showed a slight smile as he saw that it was full of Lego Star Wars pieces and figures, and eagerly began to take out the figures and examining them. He said, "Line them up!" and began to lay the figures in a straight line in front of himself.

The Challenges of AS and the Therapy Process

The scenario I have just shared is a common one, and it is becoming even more common. The diagnosis of children, adolescents, and even adults with AS is on the rise and despite the many arguments for the reasons why, these individuals are being referred to child psychologists and counselors at alarming rates. For the families of these children, there is a great sense of fear, frustration, and sadness at the difficulties that are encountered on a daily basis. For the children and adolescents, there is a sense they do not fit in, and they often feel misunderstood and are content to watch life from the sidelines (Munro, 2010). Thus, many therapists find themselves dealing with sometimes triple or quadruple issues: (a) A family unit that is under a great deal of stress, (b) a parental unit that is having difficulty coping, (c) the child or adolescent struggling with the difficulties that go along with AS, and (d) school issues that arise because of the challenges that AS presents. This is particularly true for younger children who are just beginning the school journey and have not yet received a formal diagnosis of AS, but who have several traits indicative of the syndrome.

Many therapists are trained from the vantage point that the client is going to respond to their questions or insights, and most theories and techniques are rooted in the context of a back-and-forth communication between therapist and client. With children or adolescents that fall into the Autism spectrum, this is definitely not the case. In fact, the verbal information that is shared by these individuals can sometimes be confusing or irrelevant to the therapy process. For instance, one young man that I worked with would talk incessantly about *America's Most Wanted* when given the opportunity to speak, yet he would shut down when I brought the subject of anxiety that he was originally referred for. Thus, therapists finds themselves with little or no information to go on in regards to the direction of therapy and many find parents standing with proverbial hands-on-hips waiting for progress, change, and information regarding their beloved child or adolescent. Even therapists who utilize play in their work are often baffled with a child diagnosed with AS because the therapist does not know what to do with the material from the play sessions (Munro, 2010). Later in the book I will discuss how to help parents; as well as explain why seemingly demanding and frustrating parents are really just grieving, scared, and feeling alone.

Roger Revisited

The case of Roger turned out to be very successful. But it could have turned out poorly, leaving a discouraged parent, frustrated therapist, and a child who would potentially continue through life misunderstood and stuck inside his Asperger's shell.

What did the therapist do that made the work with Roger successful? It all began with the therapeutic relationship. Even though Roger did not have the ability to communicate to the therapist his inner thoughts and feelings, he did have the ability to play. The therapist began to voice back to Roger his actions and verbal responses through behavioral tracking and reflective listening. Both of these techniques will be discussed in later sections and are very important in working with children, especially those that have social interaction difficulties. When Roger said, "Line them up!" the therapist said, "You are lining them up!" This is an example of reflective listening, a process whereby the therapist voices back what the child said. When Roger started to build something using the Lego bricks, the therapist said, "You are going to build something;" this is an example of behavioral tracking. Behavioral tracking consists of adding a commentary to the child's behavior and letting the child know that the therapist is present and is keenly aware of what the child is doing. Both of these techniques are valuable in building trust and developing a therapeutic relationship between child and therapist.

Too often, inexperienced therapists and even parents overwhelm children with a barrage of questions that do nothing more than alienate the child and impede the building of a relationship. My colleagues and I are often saddened by stories of children, particularly those in the foster care system, whose caregivers were told that counseling would be "ineffective" because the therapist assigned to the child tells the caregiver "they won't talk to me." Children who have suffered neglect or abuse of any kind are going to have serious difficulties trusting others. What makes us think that we as therapists are so special that a child is "supposed" to talk to us or that the child will even want to? This fact is especially true when working with children diagnosed with AS. Later in the book I will discuss the delicate process of building a relationship with an adolescent or child diagnosed with AS, but one thing that I must emphasize now is the importance of letting go of your "therapist agenda" and learn to "just be" with these children and adolescents.

The case of Roger was not an easy one. In fact, it took many sessions for Roger to even begin to acknowledge the therapist and to incorporate the therapist into the play sessions. It took even more sessions to continue working on the issues that were causing problems for Roger. However, over the course of time an amazing thing began to happen. Roger began to gain a sense of self, and his self-confidence began to grow. Roger's behaviors that were rooted in anxiety began to disappear, and he began to be able to interact better with peers. The therapist became an advocate for Roger at school, helping teachers to understand why he exhibited the behaviors that he did and how to help him in his education environment. Roger's mother found ways to connect better with Roger through joining in the play process and incorporating the play techniques that she observed in the therapy sessions.

A New Beginning

This is an exciting time in the world of working with young people and adults diagnosed with AS. A great deal of research of AS has been amassed in the last few years both in the scientific as well as the therapeutic realm. Researchers and practitioners, such as Simon Baron-Cohen, Richard Bromfield, Tony Attwood, and Dan LeGoff, are just a few of the amazing people who are helping parents, teachers, and therapists who come in contact with the child, adolescent, or adult diagnosed with AS to be better equipped with knowledge and skills to help these extraordinary individuals. It is an honor for me to include the work of these remarkable individuals and a humbling experience to strive to reach their level of knowledge, expertise, and skill. Still, there is much to discover about AS, and despite new knowledge, our journey is far from over.

Working with children and adolescents diagnosed with AS is a challenge—a challenge that calls for therapists who are not only trained with clinical insight and knowledge, but who are also armed with patience, empathy, and a vision to go outside the traditional boundaries of the therapeutic experience. We must be willing to step outside of the comfortable confines of therapeutic theory and let our imaginations expand. We must be willing to conduct research and share our knowledge, breaking down the walls of isolation and communicating with our colleagues. Most important, we must be thinking of the young people who live daily with the struggles that AS represents, as well as their families. If we therapists who utilize play in our work with children apply those same techniques in a context of understanding about the world of AS, we hold a great power in being able to help pull these remarkable children and adolescents up the developmental ladder.

This is my guiding passion in writing this book. I set out to write this book in a clear and simple manner, breaking down the research into more easily digested chunks but not negating the importance of such findings. The references provided contain a great deal of research information for those who hunger for an expanded and deeper search of the literature about AS. Another goal was to clearly and simply share techniques that I have utilized in my work with these gifted children and adolescents. I set out to demystify the therapy process for students or novice therapists who are just beginning their journey in helping children and adolescents diagnosed with AS and also to provide valuable techniques and insight for seasoned professionals looking to add to their repertoire of skills. My ultimate goal is to add to the knowledge base for those in the helping professions who work with children and adolescents diagnosed with AS and fill a gap in the literature.

The following chapters are going to help you, the therapist, use play therapy in helping solve the puzzle of providing therapeutic services to those affected by AS. Do not forget the journey of helping a young person with AS will test you, yet the journey will yield greater understanding of yourself as well as in those with which you are working. I have found that working with these amazing young people has made me a much better person, husband, father, and friend; not just a better therapist. I cannot tell you how many times I leave my office at the end of the day amazed by a keen observation of one of the children or adolescents diagnosed with AS that I am so honored to meet. Together, all of us can help enhance the lives of these amazing young people, and help them realize their full potential.

Chapter 2

What Is Asperger's Syndrome?

THE HISTORY OF AS

The traits that comprise AS were first identified by a Viennese child psychiatrist named Hans Asperger. In 1944, Asperger published a paper in which he described a group of male children who had difficulties with social and emotional integration, in addition to exhibiting "egocentric preoccupation with unusual and circumscribed interests" (Weber, 2008, p. 15). Asperger also noted conversational deficiencies in the boy's conversations which lacked reciprocal sharing of information and contained unembellished, straight-forward interpretations that tend to be hallmark symptoms of AS. Sadly, Asperger's paper was not translated into English for many years, and it was not until Lorna Wing's article *AS: A Clinical Account* in 1981 that the term "Asperger's Syndrome" was introduced into the English language. Wing, an English psychiatrist and physician who raised a daughter diagnosed with autism, has spent many years researching autism and AS (Wing, 2005).

Uta Frith, a developmental psychologist, translated Asperger's original paper into English in 1991, which had an immediate, worldwide impact on clinicians and parents (Frith, 1991). Frith's translation and Wing's clinical work were instrumental in the inclusion of AS in both the DSM-IV and ICD-10 in 1994 (Volkmar, Klin, Siegel, Szatmari, Lord, and Campbell, 1994) and gave AS inclusion in the autistic spectrum. An ongoing debate, which has yet to be resolved, is whether or not AS should be included in the autistic spectrum or stand alone as a separate, unique condition (Baron-Cohen, 2006). In fact, at the time of this writing, the American Psychological Association is considering doing away with AS as a separate form of autism for the upcoming DSM-V and instead including it under one category along with Autism.

7

The purported reasoning behind this change is based on research that AS and classic Autism do not have enough differences to divide them. However many professionals disagree with this, citing that to remove the separate category of AS from the Autism spectrum at this time would be detrimental to those who have found a name that specifically details the symptoms that comprise the way these individuals think and behave (Baron-Cohen, 2009). Regardless of whether the APA decides to include AS in the new DSM or not, the proliferation of many books and research articles provide a foundation for improved understanding of this unique and fascinating world and demand that teachers, clinicians, and researchers continue to work to better understand individuals diagnosed with AS. As the knowledge of AS continues to grow, the adults, children, teens, and families and the clinicians who serve them form a cohesive unit in seeking to find balance in living with AS and overcoming the challenges.

ASPERGER'S SYNDROME AND DIAGNOSTIC CRITERIA

The following information comes from the American Psychological Association's *Diagnostic and Statistical Manual of Mental Disorders* (DSM-IV TR, 2000).

A. Qualitative impairment in social interaction, as manifested by at least two of the following:
   • Marked impairment in the use of multiple non-verbal behaviors such as eye-to-eye gaze, facial expressions, body postures, and gestures to regulate social interaction
   • Failure to develop peer relationships appropriate to developmental level
   • A lack of spontaneous seeking to share enjoyment, interests, or achievements with other people (e.g., by a lack of showing, bringing, or pointing out objects of interest to other people)
   • Lack social or emotional reciprocity
B. Restricted, repetitive and stereotyped patterns of behavior, interests, and activities, as manifested by at least one of the following:
   • Encompassing preoccupations with one or more stereotyped and restricted patterns of interest that is abnormal either in intensity or focus
   • Apparently inflexible adherence to specific nonfunctional routines or rituals
   • Stereotyped and repetitive motor mannerisms (e.g., hand or finger flapping or twisting, or complex whole-body movements)

- Persistent preoccupation with parts of objects
C. The disturbance causes clinically significant impairment in social, occupational, or other important areas of functioning
D. There is no clinically significant delay in language (single words used by age 2 years, communicative phrases used by 3 years)
E. There is no clinically significant delay in cognitive development or in the development of age-appropriate self-help skills, adaptive behavior (other than in social interaction), and curiosity about the environment in childhood.
F. Criteria are not met for another specific PDD or schizophrenia. (APA, 2000).

Some people who work closely with individuals diagnosed with AS believe that the DSM-IV-TR diagnosis is lacking because it does not include the speech and language difficulties that Hans Asperger noted in his original work. While I do not want to get into a debate regarding diagnostic criteria, I do want to include the criteria of Gillberg (1991) because I believe it is important to include the sections regarding speech and language difficulties that are common in individuals diagnosed with AS. Following is the criteria for AS that Gillberg (1991) proposed.

1. Severe impairment in reciprocal social interaction (at least two of the following)
   (a) Inability to interact with peers
   (b) Lack of desire to interact with peers
   (c) Lack of appreciation of social cues
   (d) Socially and emotionally inappropriate behavior
2. All-absorbing narrow interest (at least one of the following)
   (a) Exclusion of other activities
   (b) Repetitive adherence
   (c) More rote than meaning
3. Imposition of routines and interests (at least one of the following)
   (a) On self, in aspects of life
   (b) On others
4. Speech and language problems (at least three of the following)
   (a) Delayed development
   (b) Superficially perfect expressive language
   (c) Formal, pedantic language
   (d) Odd prosody, peculiar voice characteristics
   (e) Impairment of comprehension including misinterpretations of literal or implied meanings

5. *Non-verbal communication problems (at least one of the following)*
   (a) Limited use of gestures
   (b) Clumsy/gauche body language
   (c) Limited facial expression
   (d) Inappropriate expression
   (e) Peculiar, stiff gaze
6. *Motor clumsiness:* poor performance on neurodevelopmental examination

ADDITIONAL SYMPTOMS EXPANDED UPON

In addition to the clinical criteria, there are often other symptoms that are reported by parents/caregivers, teachers, or other people involved in the person's life. The specific treatment of these symptoms using play therapy will be addressed later in the book. One of these additional symptoms is preoccupation with special interests. Many of the young people that I work with exhibit intense and focused energy on things like Pokemon, various video games (RuneScape, World of Warcraft), movies and TV shows. Another additional symptom is a stiff, plodding, one-sided conversation style. For the person who has not experienced talking with a person who has AS, this feature can make one very frustrated, and many family members (especially mothers) tell me with tears in their eyes of giving up and letting the young person ramble on and on, not knowing how to stop them. Yet another symptom is the appearance of a lack of empathy for others' feelings. This not only frustrates parents and teachers, but also can strike terror in parents' hearts as they think of possible future ramifications of not being able to show empathy such as being incarcerated or socially rejected.

A problematic symptom that often exists is a negative, pessimistic world view. This can take caregivers, teachers, and peers by surprise as the young persons with AS voice their often downbeat and depressing view of how they see life. It is no wonder that these individuals appear to be very depressed in addition to having other difficulties. Along with the difficulty in relating socially with peers of the same age, young people diagnosed with AS often have difficulty in expressing themselves and interpreting their own feelings. I discuss later in the book how the therapist must be able to listen carefully and not be too quick to apply a judgment on the young person's interpretation of an event. If the therapist is wrong, it can result in the young person shutting down or feeling threatened.

ASPERGER'S SYNDROME IN MODERN MENTAL HEALTH AND EDUCATION

Hans Asperger could not have known how large an influence his paper would have, not only in medicine, mental health, and education, but also in everyday, popular culture. Since the early 1980s, literally hundreds of scholarly books and articles have been written on AS, just in the academic realm alone. In1981 the computer database of the National Autistic Society listed only two publications that mentioned AS but by 2004 that number rose to over 900 (Wing, 2005). This proliferation of information has been helpful in training therapists, counselors, and educators to work with children, teens, and adults who have been diagnosed with AS. The internet has abounded with information about AS, and countless websites have sprung up designed to help the professional clinician, the struggling family, or the average lay person better understand the world of AS.

Educational professionals such as teachers, school counselors, and school psychologists have been put in the position of helping young people diagnosed with AS succeed in school. As a result of the increase in public awareness as well as an increase in diagnosis, school professionals found themselves scrambling to understand these children and adolescents, to meet their educational needs, and incorporate them into the mainstream teaching climate. One of the most frustrating dynamics for educators is the asynchrony of normal to high intelligence, yet the fragile, emotionally immature, and socially inept AS child or adolescent. These characteristics often result in bullying of the AS child or adolescent, which can lead to further emotional damage and social withdrawal. Another question surrounds placement. Where is the best placement for the AS child in the learning environment? Is the AS child to be in the gifted program or the mainstream? How does the educator help educate given the difficulties with socialization? These questions create frustrations for the parents, teacher, and the child or adolescent diagnosed with AS.

ASPERGER'S SYNDROME IN MODERN CULTURE

In recent years, there has been a dramatic increase in the portrayal of AS in mainstream culture. Recent films such as *Mozart and the Whale, Adam,* and *Thinking in Pictures* are just a few examples of major films that intrigued the general public about AS. The general public's interest in AS is often piqued by the eccentric and odd characters that are displayed, generating both potentially positive and negative results. The interest has a positive effect by creating awareness of the people who live with Asperger's and helping others to see them as basically normal individuals who tend to have quirky behaviors based on their difficulties with social interactions.

In fact, many persons living with AS now refer to themselves as "Aspies," or "Aspergians," which implies self-acceptance and empowerment due to the individual being neither ashamed nor inhibited in letting others know of the condition with which they live. An example of this is Temple Grandin, who through her books exemplifies how someone who lives with the challenges of AS can overcome those challenges and turn the challenges into strengths. Another example is John Elder Robison, whose book *Look Me in the Eye* (which will be discussed in more detail in Chapter Three) provides a wonderful, empowering autobiographical account of his life that details the twists and turns of the challenges, yet blessings of life with AS. These stories can help not only in educating the general public about the various challenges that a person with AS can face, creating empathy and understanding, but I have found they give parents, children, adolescents, and adults living with AS hope and encouragement.

Potentially detrimental to the cause of AS awareness are the sensationalized exaggerations sometimes portrayed in movies and television shows which can leave people thinking that all individuals diagnosed with AS are mean, superintelligent beings who possess amazing mental powers and abilities. While there are individuals diagnosed with AS who possess higher intelligence and remarkable cognitive abilities, many are of average intelligence and do not have a specific area in which they exhibit particularly masterful tendencies. Like one adolescent who came to me remarked, "I am just an average person, I guess, but I just see the world from a different spaceship."

While many individuals with AS struggle with social interactions and may display awkwardness in social situations, it does not mean they are mean-spirited or are rude to every person they meet. As "neurotypicals" (the name that those diagnosed with AS give to those who do not have the characteristics of AS) we must remember that just as people without AS have a range of intelligence, personality traits, interests, and abilities, individuals with AS have ranges of these same factors even though the characteristics displayed for diagnosis are the same. I have yet to meet two individuals diagnosed with AS who are exactly the same in interest, personality, or abilities, yet the traits that warrant the diagnosis in these children, adolescents, and adults are very similar.

Chapter 3

Potential Challenges of Therapy with Children and Adolescents Diagnosed with Asperger's Syndrome

OVERVIEW

There are some potential challenges that a therapist may encounter when working with children or adolescents. Not all of these will be encountered with every child or adolescent diagnosed with AS, but they are common. I feel that being aware of these is useful to the therapist seeking to work with children or adolescents diagnosed with AS because, as I have mentioned earlier, this work will be challenging, both mentally and emotionally. Therapists must be prepared to modify their approaches and not get discouraged in working with clients diagnosed with AS. Therapists must be prepared to be encouragers and educators for family members and caregivers.

SOCIAL AND CONVERSATIONAL BARRIERS

For anyone who has come in contact with a child or adolescent diagnosed with AS, there are noticeable traits and differences that set the child or adolescent apart from neurotypical children. It is no wonder, then, that the clinician who encounters a child or adolescent diagnosed with AS, can often feel lost and confused when trying to begin making a connection. Most traditional forms of therapy rely on the ability of the client or patient to respond to the therapist's questions in the form of fully or at least half-organized verbal responses.

In addition, the whole context of traditional therapy with both children and adults assumes that the client or patient understands and exists in the social and cultural climate of the therapist. The client or patient, whether adult, child, couple, or family, along with the therapist tends to be on the same social and cultural page. Another way of thinking of this is to imagine that everyone is watching the same movie and sees the same thing, gets the plot, and for the most part comes away with the same experience. Now imagine that the movie that you are watching is completely different from the one that everyone else is watching. Your movie has parts that are funny during the times that everyone else's movie is sad; and when everyone else is laughing hysterically the movie you are watching is not funny at all. In addition, the themes, ideas, and social and cultural imagery in your movie is not present nor understood by everyone else, because they are watching a completely different movie. Thus, when the child or adolescent diagnosed with AS enters the therapy office, it is not only unfamiliar and potentially anxiety provoking, but it does not fit into a mental, emotional, or social context.

The therapy office can often be unnerving for any child or adolescent, whether they are diagnosed with AS or not, and I often remind parents that their child is actually "normal" for feeling some level of anxiety or being resistant to the initial prospect of therapy. One adolescent diagnosed with AS shared with me his initial thought process when he met me for the first time two years prior:

> Well, when my parents told me that I HAD to go and talk with someone, my initial thought was that I had done something wrong and that for sure there was something wrong with me. I don't like new places and meeting new people was always scary, and one more opportunity for me to screw up. Almost like, almost like a set up. I mean, I know that my parents love me and all, but new people and places never . . . like never fit right. So . . . I was really nervous so I just didn't talk to you at all.

Most therapists who work with children and adolescents expect some resistance initially, however, most are NOT used to being completely ignored and dismissed without any eye contact and non-verbal communication. There is also a fundamental social expectation in American society that a child MUST communicate with an adult when the adult asks them a question and look them directly in the eye, and to not do so is considered grave disrespect. John Elder Robinson in *Look Me in the Eye* speaks of his difficulties as a child and his inability to make eye contact:

> "Look me in the eye, young man!" I cannot tell you how many times I heard that shrill, whining refrain. It started about the time I got to first grade. I heard it from parents, relatives, teachers, principals, and all manner of other people. I heard it so often I began to expect to hear it. Sometimes it would be punctuated by a jab from a ruler of one of those rubber-tipped pointers teachers used in

those days. The teachers would say, "Look at me when I'm speaking to you!" I would squirm and continue looking at the floor, which would just make them madder. I would glance up at their hostile faces and feel squirmier and more uncomfortable and unable to form words, and I would quickly look away (Robinson, 2007, 2008, p. 1).

In addition, Robinson (2007, 2008) makes the following statement: "Everyone thought they understood my behavior. They thought it was simple: I was just no good.

"Nobody trusts a man who won't look them in the eye."
"You look like a criminal."
"You're up to something. I know it!" (p. 2).

I bring this up because psychologists, counselors, and teachers are not immune to the effects of social expectations that place these cultural demands on young people and often therapists do not realize how conditioned they have become despite years of clinical practice and training. The therapist who is working with a child or adolescent diagnosed with AS must accept the lack of traditional verbal/social reciprocity that is often exhibited and work to become comfortable with this aspect of working with this population.

HURRY UP AND WAIT: RELATIONSHIP BARRIERS

As a result of seeing the world differently and having difficulties with conversation, children and adolescents diagnosed with AS have problems forming relationships with peers and adults. Neurotypical individuals tend to possess the ability from a very early age to foster relationships through eye contact and reciprocal facial movements, and as a young person ages, this ability continues to expand as they develop mentally, emotionally, and physically. For the child diagnosed with AS, the signals continue to get crossed, and the learning process that normally develops is disrupted and delayed, leaving caregivers confused by the lack of conversational and social reciprocity.

One identified problem that contributes to these signals becoming crossed and resulting in social deficiencies is the deficit in joint attention. Joint attention is defined as the behaviors that a child uses to direct the attention of another person to an object of interest (Baron-Cohen, 1999) and these behaviors include "the pointing gesture, gaze-monitoring, and showing gestures, most of which are absent in most children with autism" (p. 14). Joint attention is very important in connecting to another person and is an essential building block in forming and maintaining relationships. Researchers have shown that joint attention deficits are precursors to a lack of development of other pieces that are important in developing social skills and forming relationships (Baron-Cohen, 1999).

Neurotypical individuals tend to build relationships by observing and predicting safe, repetitive behaviors, such as eye contact, gestures, and voice recognition. The child diagnosed with AS stays in egocentric toddler mode socially, assuming that all adults and surrounding persons in the environment are there to simply attend to them. Two terms that capture this phenomenon are "mindblindness" and "alexithymia." Mindblindness is a term that describes the inability of the person diagnosed with AS to foresee and understand the intentions of others (Baron-Cohen, 1995). Alexithymia is known as the inability to recognize and give meaning to emotional signals in oneself and others (Fitzgerald and Bellgrove, 2006). These two characteristics create difficulties for the individual diagnosed with AS in building and maintaining relationships as well as in relation to insight and emotional control, and they cause major challenges for the therapist.

Therapists are trained to build relationships, and the therapeutic relationship which contains the core element of trust is recognized as the catalyst in producing change in a child or adolescent. However, children and adolescents diagnosed with AS have difficulty building relationships and learning to trust unfamiliar people. This presents a difficult barrier for the therapist who must be able to recognize the barrier, understand it, and overcome it. The relationship difficulties are compounded by either the walled silence of the child or adolescent who simply does not do well connecting with strange people or the incessant chattering of the child or adolescent diagnosed with AS who does trust the therapist but who, through no fault of their own, has their own agenda of what information will be shared.

OBSESSIVE THINKING AND RESTRICTED INTERESTS

One of the characteristics of individuals diagnosed with AS is the intensity toward restricted interests that manifest in obsessive thinking and repeated conversation and behavior. When someone meets an individual diagnosed with AS for the first time, the knowledge that the individual holds on a particular subject can be quite impressive, until one realizes that the knowledge base rests totally on the one subject or idea and in other areas the individual diagnosed with AS is virtually ignorant. This ignorance is not because of a defect in learning. It is selective because in the individual's brain new information is labeled as "not interesting" and is not included in the topics that the individual diagnosed with AS wants to investigate or discuss. It is helpful to imagine a power-saving device on a machine to illustrate this. The device allows only the minimum amount of power to conserve energy, and so that only the most vital parts of the machine are used so as to not waste power or wear out parts prematurely. The child or adolescent "shuts off" parts of the brain that take in information that the child or adolescent deems "boring" or "unnecessary," thus conserving the brain's energy for what the child or adolescent does find interesting.

For instance, one young man in one of my social skills groups could only talk about sports, and as long as the topic at hand to discuss related to sports in some way, he was active and involved. As soon as another topic was brought up such as music or a movie not relating to sports, he would clear his throat angrily, take deep breaths, and mutter something like "This is utterly ridiculous!" One-track thinking and conversation create huge barriers in the building of the therapeutic relationship because the child or adolescent diagnosed with AS will begin by discussing those topics that they are interested in, and as soon as the therapist begins to explore another area, the child or adolescent either shuts down or rambles on completely unaware of the therapist's desire to change the topic.

One young man that I worked with tended to be obsessed with *America's Most Wanted* and would not only watch the latest episode but would record it and then watch it close to 50 times during the week. This was in addition to checking the website each hour to get updates on any reported sightings or arrests of the individuals portrayed on the show. Each week he would observe individuals at the mall and in the town in which we live just in case he saw anyone that matched the description that was portrayed on the show. As our therapy sessions began, it became difficult to talk with him because he would talk about nothing other than the show. I would begin to guide our conversation to another topic such as school or family, and he would wait until I had asked my question and then began right again to focus on *America's Most Wanted.* This can be frustrating for a therapist and I will discuss techniques later in the book to help with situations such as this.

RESISTANCE TO INSIGHT-ORIENTED THERAPIES

One more barrier that is created in the therapy room in working with children and adolescents with AS is the lack of effectiveness of insight-oriented approaches because of the lack of perspective-taking (theory of mind) that often accompanies individuals diagnosed with AS. Many therapy approaches rely on the ability of the child, adolescent, or adult to have insight into their behaviors, which the therapist capitalizes on to help the individual change their behaviors. For instance, if a child who hits others when frustrated can be shown that hitting another child is painful and connect to the idea that they, the hitter, would not like to be hit, more than likely that child who is hitting is going to stop doing the hitting based on this insight. However, for most children and adolescents diagnosed with AS, there is an inability to see things from another's view, which creates a huge barrier in getting the child or adolescent diagnosed with AS to change a behavior or gain a new social skill. Mindblindness creates deficits in empathy and sympathy which are key ingredients in understanding the intentions of others and being able to predict the behavior of others in relationships.

For instance, many children or adolescents diagnosed with AS struggle with hygiene, which is very frustrating to many parents. I encounter several frustrated parents who come into my office and tell me how they have tried to get their child or adolescent diagnosed with AS to improve their hygiene through insight-oriented means, such as telling them they stink, or attempting to shame them into brushing their teeth or bathing. I help them see that because of the inability to see things from another's perspective, those approaches will not work. For the therapist, they must have the ability to focus on helping parents with behavioral approaches for problematic situations like hygiene mentioned above, and utilize a different approach therapeutically with the child or teen.

IMPATIENT PARENTS AND UNREALISTIC PARENTAL EXPECTATIONS

Sometimes the parents of the child or adolescent diagnosed with AS can become a barrier because of being desperate to find a way to make their children "normal." These parents often don't understand the time that it takes to build a relationship with a child or adolescent diagnosed with AS, and are unfamiliar with therapy approaches that need to be modified to effectively work with these young people. There is a great need for the therapist to be an educator/encourager/advocate for the parents and family members of those diagnosed with AS, so that they can better understand the process and be vested in the process. Some of the barriers that can potentially arise are parents/caregivers who are resistant to the process of therapy because of not seeing expected results, parents/caregivers who give up on various behavioral techniques that need to be followed at home, or parents/caregivers who simply remove the child or adolescent from the therapy process. Most difficult situations with parents/caregivers can be cleared up by a therapist who communicates effectively about the therapy process and seeks to inform the parents/caregivers and encourages them. We must remember that it is the parents and caregivers who are on the front lines with the child or adolescent diagnosed with AS and the therapist must not take it personally when these parents and caregivers voice their frustrations, or push the therapist to provide explanations about why it seems that "things are not getting better." In these situations, it is imperative that the therapist listen, let the parent(s) know that the therapist hears them, and seek to educate the parent/caregiver further and provide coping skills for the parent or caregiver and the rest of the family.

Chapter 4

The Therapeutic Alliance, Empathy, and Themes in Play Therapy with Children Diagnosed with Asperger's Syndrome

THE THERAPEUTIC ALLIANCE

I will discuss briefly the therapeutic alliance when working with children and adolescents diagnosed with AS. As I mentioned in Chapter Three, building the therapeutic alliance with a child or adolescent diagnosed with AS can be difficult if the therapist has not encountered this type of client before. The therapeutic alliance is seen by many theorists, researchers, and practitioners as being the very foundation of therapeutic work with any client in any setting, but especially with children and adolescents (Ackerman and Hilsenroth, 2003; Crenshaw and Mordock, 2005; Saunders, 2001). The therapeutic alliance sets the stage for further therapeutic work and embeds a foundation of trust and safety (Crenshaw and Mordock, 2005).

When working with children and adolescents diagnosed with AS, the therapeutic alliance is even more important given the barriers and emotional walls that the therapist is likely to have to overcome (Jacobsen, 2004). I believe that to build a solid therapeutic alliance with children and adolescents diagnosed with AS means that I must be patient, and be truly in awe of the person who sits before me. I must throw out an agenda of what I believe to be progress and simply focus on just being in the presence of the child or adolescent diagnosed with AS. I must seek with all my being and ability to concentrate and focus on the words, behavior, and mannerisms in order to enter the child or teen's world. Only then can I begin to understand and connect and allow the child or adolescent to experience the safety and serenity that will lead to the establishment of trust. As I mentioned earlier, I have yet to meet two children or adolescents diagnosed with AS that have the same personality, gifts, interests, or abilities. Each is unique, and each requires me to be open, curious, present, and focused as I attempt to see the world through their eyes and develop empathy for the amazing young person sitting before me.

TECHNIQUES TO BUILD THE THERAPEUTIC ALLIANCE WITH CHILDREN AND ADOLESCENTS DIAGNOSED WITH ASPERGER'S SYNDROME

"Just Be"

I cannot emphasize the concept of "just be" enough when I discuss the concept of building the therapeutic alliance with children and adolescents diagnosed with AS. To "just be" means that I am not reactive or pushy, impatient, or controlling. It means that I am willing to just observe and participate in a patient, non-threatening manner. This concept is akin to the therapist being an explorer to a new land: There is a background of knowledge and skill that the explorer brings to the discovery, yet he or she is in the process of uncovering and experiencing the new place by immersing him/herself into the new place. By being non-reactive and maintaining an open and non-threatening stance, the therapist is demonstrating to the patient that the office and the therapist are safe. It must be remembered that the child diagnosed with AS has already come to see the world as dangerous and frightening, and many have a very hard time with a new place that is not related to home or school. Therefore, expect some resistance and guarded behavior. Another part of the therapist "just being" is to be curious, patient, and gentle, allowing the child to explore in a curious way.

Get Comfortable with Silence

Children and adolescents diagnosed with AS can be quite verbal once they are comfortable with a person or place, but in the beginning the child or adolescent can appear to be in shut-down mode. As discussed earlier, the therapist must learn to not panic here, simply observe and be patient. It is fine to ask a question, but if no response is offered, just wait. When a child or adolescent diagnosed with AS does not respond, it does not mean that the therapist is being ignored, it can mean that the question is being processed or that the child is testing the environment or the therapist for safety. I once saw an interview with Roger Waters of the legendary band Pink Floyd and he shared that the blank spaces in music, the spacing, makes the music more beautiful and powerful. It is what we do not hear in the music that can be just as beautiful as what we do hear, and the spacing prepares us for the sound, and it is received with a grateful ear. I believe that the same is true for spaces of silence in communicating with others and especially in the dialogue process of the therapeutic relationship. Silence not only allows for the testing of safety by the child or adolescent diagnosed with AS but also for the rhythm of connection and understanding to be established.

One of the first young people diagnosed with AS that I ever worked with (his case will be discussed later in the section on adolescents) taught me much in this area. As we began working together, I started to fire questions at him. When I did not get a response, I began to ask more questions. Feeling frustrated, I invited him to play a game of chess, something that his parents told me that he liked. I opened the box and set up the pieces. Again, he gave me no response and would not even look at me. I then quickly grabbed some paper and invited him to draw. He stared at the blank paper, becoming visibly upset. Knowing that he loved nature and outdoors, I invited him to walk along the lake that was near my office. He pumped his head up and down in an emphatic "YES!" and we headed outside. He walked so quickly I had to run to keep up with him, but gradually he slowed down, and we finished the session with me asking questions every few minutes but continuing to get no response. The second, third, and fourth sessions continued the same way, with us walking/running around the lake but I began to ask fewer and fewer questions. Finally, at the fifth session, I was determined to say nothing at all—no questions, no observations, nothing; just my presence would suffice. We began to walk/run and he instantly slowed when I did not say anything. We got about halfway around the lake and he gave me a look that said, "Okay, you finally got it" and began to answer virtually every question that I had asked in those first four sessions. Years later he explained to me that my initial approach "overwhelmed" him and reminded him of the way teachers and other authority figures would bombard him with tasks, questions, and procedures that took his brain awhile to comprehend.

Use of Behavioral Tracking

Behavioral tracking is often discussed in child-therapy literature (Van Velsor, 2004) and is a technique used to reflect content and meaning in the child's play behavior in the therapy room. "In behavioral tracking, the counselor simply reflects to the child what he or she is doing at any particular moment" (Van Velsor, 2004, p. 313). I have found this technique useful when working with children who have verbalization difficulties, particularly those diagnosed with AS. Because of the verbal, relational, and interactional barriers and difficulties, this technique can help build the therapeutic alliance as well as increase the child or teen's sense of safety. The therapist who models behavioral tracking is saying to the child "I am here with you and I am paying attention to you, and you are important." For example, when a child is beginning to build with a set of blocks, the therapist would say, "You have found the blocks and you are going to build with them." Then, as the child begins to build a structure, the therapist would say, "Now you have built a house" (or tower, or whatever building the therapist believes it to be). The child may not respond at all during this time, but the therapist is allowing the child to know that the therapist is part of the action. I often have students who voice concerns that he or she will interpret the wrong meaning of the child's play in behavioral tracking and I reassure the student that most of the time the child will tell you if you are off. For example, if the therapist said, "Now you are building a house," the child might loudly say, "It's a jail, not a house!" This serves to give the child a chance to know that they are allowed to verbalize, which can provide a sense of safety and empowerment and keeps the therapist on target regarding the intent of the child's play.

When Invited to Join in the Play, Follow Directions!

During the trust building stage of therapy, the child will often invite the therapist to play with him/her. I feel this is very important, and if invited, the therapist should take the plunge. The first reason the invitation is important is that it helps to establish trust between therapist and the child and creates a foundation that can lead toward change later on. Second, this invitation is an opening for the therapist to gain insight into the thoughts and emotions of the child. Children diagnosed with AS tend to be very precise in their play and for those with OCD tendencies, even more so. For this reason, the child diagnosed with AS will often be very directive in play, and I have encountered them to be quite clear regarding how they want me to join them. The therapist should join the play and follow the directions of the child diagnosed with AS and if there is a question, just ask them and most of the time the child will reply.

For example, a young girl that I worked with loved to play with a castle and Lego horses. She would also involve a stuffed blue bird from a basket of stuffed animals. One day during the third session in which I was watching her play, she saw that I was observing her and she told me quite emphatically to "take the brown horses over to that chair." "Is this someone's castle?" I asked. "No, that is where the bad person takes the horses and then the blue bird is going to rescue them." I asked her what I should do next and she then told me to wait until she gave the order, and then later told me to take the brown horses somewhere else "where they will be safe." This scenario was played out each session and I became more and more involved in the sessions.

Let Your Imagination Be a Part of the Process

When I first received training in play therapy, there was a part of me that leaped up and down like a child, and I felt something awake in me that had been sleeping for a while. I realized later that it was my imagination. I find that most people stop "playing" by the time they reach the age of twelve. Even for those who play a sport, it is around this age that the young athlete receives the message that they now must become "serious" about their sport. While I was very excited to learn about play therapy and utilizing this amazing approach to therapy, I was also very concerned about "messing up." I read the books, the manuals, and tentatively and cautiously would enter the play-therapy world with the child. Of course, this is how any fledgling therapist starts out, afraid of causing irreparable damage to the people who have come for help. However, at some point the therapist must leave the book, manual, or journal on the desk and get down on the floor and *do* play therapy. This is where the imagination enters the picture. I want to encourage the reader that working with children and adolescents diagnosed with AS is "outside the box" much of the time because these astonishing young people are "outside the box," and imagination is a key element in connecting and helping them. Research, clinical training and ethics are important components; but play is about imagination. Working with children and adolescents who struggle with exploratory and spontaneous play requires someone who is willing to imagine for them and imagine with them. I challenge the reader to gain as much training as possible and to read and study all the facets of play therapy they can get their hands on, but remember to be imaginative and to let the imaginative part of your being gel with your clinical self as you work with these remarkable young people.

EMPATHY

Many authors have written about the importance of empathy in the creation of the therapeutic alliance (Bennet, 2001; Crenshaw and Hardy, 2007), and I believe firmly in the power of empathy as a necessary ingredient in working with children and adolescents diagnosed with AS. Living in a world where they are misunderstood, bullied, and rejected, children and adolescents diagnosed with AS require an empathic, patient, and gentle therapist with which to form a therapeutic bond. Building the therapeutic alliance takes time, and the barriers that exist when attempting to bond with children and adolescents diagnosed with AS can potentially make the bonding/trust stage even longer. In a world of managed care and a culture that demands results in shorter and shorter amounts of time, a therapist is often pressured to focus on techniques and ignore elements such as empathy that lead to a therapeutic bond. Crenshaw and Hardy (2007) discuss how the lack of empathy disrupts the ability of the therapist to form a therapeutic bond with the child because there is a lack of trust on the part of the child or teen. Without this trust, the child or adolescent may remain aloof and distant. Parents, the foster care system, or other governing bodies who can often expect instant results can make the mistake of deeming the therapy process "non-productive" and eventually abandon it altogether. This danger exists for the therapist who works with children and adolescents diagnosed with AS. The therapist may become frustrated by the lack of progress, but it is important that the therapist continues to display empathy for the child or adolescent that is before them and to educate the parents and caregivers about the importance of the therapeutic alliance.

THEMES IN PLAY THERAPY WITH CHILDREN DIAGNOSED WITH ASPERGER'S SYNDROME

While the themes covered here are not an exhaustive list, they represent the most common issues found in the literature and that I have encountered in my work and with children diagnosed with AS. I want to emphasize that I also have included some family considerations because I am a strong proponent of strengthening the family unit when working with children who have special needs, like the ones diagnosed with AS. Research has shown that when the family unit is strong and has coping skills, the life of the child diagnosed with AS becomes easier. Stress kills not only individuals, but it kills our families as well by shutting down the family members' ability to love, receive love, communicate, and share another's presence without being reactive, anxious, or depressed. Chapter Five will discuss the application of play therapy toys and techniques for each theme discussed here.

Theme One: Fear

As I mentioned earlier, children who are diagnosed with AS often have many fears. Some of the more common triggers for children and adolescents diagnosed with AS are related to change. Some examples of change that can cause fear are changes in routine that the child or adolescent is accustomed to as well as changes in expectations, and social situations (Attwood, 1998). Russell and Sofronoff (2005) state "Many children with AS experience difficulty with change because they have poor comprehension of occurrences in their surroundings, resulting in uncertainty and anxiety" (p. 633). The observable effects of these fears manifest themselves in the stereotypical repetitive behaviors of children diagnosed with AS such as hand flapping, rituals, echolalia, or tantrums which can be viewed as either outcomes of anxiety or attempts to cope when the child is feeling overwhelmed. Children diagnosed with AS have been found to have higher rates of fears of physical injury, separation anxiety, panic and agoraphobia, and obsessive-compulsive disorder (OCD) (Russell and Sofronoff, 2005).

It is not uncommon for children with higher levels of intelligence to have more fears than peers of average intelligence, and children and adolescents diagnosed with AS often possess higher intelligence than peers. Fears can be reinforced by the family system in that the family finds it is easier to allow the behaviors and beliefs that underlie the fears than to endure the behavioral and emotional outbursts that often accompany a thwarted ritual or belief related to a fear. For instance, one young man I worked with was afraid to leave the house. He had become a recluse, completing his school requirements in home-school format on the computer. His parents said that if they tried to make him leave the house the young man would scream and lash out physically, trying to hurt them and his peers. I was dismayed to find that his parents and siblings had accepted the fact that it was fine for him to stay inside because, they reasoned, his tantrums were so intense that the family was afraid of him in this state. They had no skills or tools to deal with their son's tantrums other than enable him to continue to draw further and further from society. This is an example of how families can keep the child or adolescent diagnosed with AS stuck in a cycle of fear.

Theme Two: Social and Relational Difficulties

I mentioned in previous chapters that social and relational difficulties are one of the main struggles for people diagnosed with AS. For children diagnosed with AS, social and relational problems can be the trigger for the caregivers to seek professional help. For parents and caregivers this is perhaps the most frustrating part of living with and caring for a child diagnosed with AS. Parents and caregivers become frustrated not only due to the lack of relationship with their son or daughter, but because of the social embarrassment and difficulties that come with a child who struggles to fit into society's social network and structure. The social and relational difficulties can spawn ridicule, rejection, and bullying; which can result in low self-worth, isolation and withdrawal, and an overall negative outlook towards themselves and life in general. Mindblindness, alexithymia, and deficits in joint attention prevent the child diagnosed with AS from successfully navigating his or her social environment and understanding the reactions and emotions of others

(Baron-Cohen, 1995; Fitzgerald and Bellgrove, 2006); and the lack of insight to comprehend their own social and emotional deficits creates enormous hurdles for the child diagnosed with AS (Russell and Sofronoff, 2005).

Theme Three: Low Self Worth

Children diagnosed with AS can become the target of intense bullying and often experience rejection by peers. Mindblindness, alexithymia, and deficits in joint attention create an inability for the child diagnosed with AS to function socially and disrupt the building of relationships. As a result, peers tend to the view the child diagnosed with AS as awkward, unpredictable, and one-dimensional in their interests. The perseveration on one interest (Pokemon, Star Wars, etc.) and the intensity of the interest appears strange to peers of the child diagnosed with AS. Neurotypical children have interests similar to children diagnosed with AS, but there tends to be a limit to the perseveration and intensity, and usually the neurotypical child is more "well-rounded" and tends to have a range of interests. It must be remembered that individuals diagnosed with AS do desire relationships with others, but it is the not knowing how to go about it that causes difficulties. Many children diagnosed with AS also demonstrate emotional inflexibility resulting in tantrums and acting out which further alienates peers (Carter, 2009).

The rejection and bullying of the child diagnosed with AS has a devastating effect on the child's mental and emotional development that results in low self-worth. The developing brain has several parts that are involved in the socialization process from the amygdala to the mid and forebrain areas (Baron-Cohen, 2006). Brain researchers have long known that repeated firing of the fight-or-flight system due to the brain's ongoing interpretation of threat creates conditioned internal and external responses manifested in negativistic thinking and acting out behaviors as the individual tries to remain safe (Rothschild, 2000). When I work with children diagnosed with AS who exhibit emotional inflexibility through tantrum behavior, I explain to the parents/caregivers/teachers that the child is in fight-or-flight mode and the root of the behavior is fear and the child believing that he or she is not safe. The child is not "bad," "oppositional-defiant," or "manipulative"; the child's brain is telling the child that they are not in a safe place and that there is danger. Thus, the child is doing what any of us would do if we believed we are in danger: Get away from the threat or fight the threat.

Continued rejection of the child by peers results in the child's perception that they are not worthy, valuable, or wanted and results in sadness, depression, and self-loathing (Carter, 2009). The residue of bullying and social rejection becomes embedded into the child's internal processes which results in withdrawal, isolation, and feelings of loneliness that the child carries well into their adult years (Baron-Cohen, 2000). I have talked with many adults diagnosed with AS who shared stories of extreme bullying in childhood which led to feelings of depression and suicidal thinking. These scars and wounds are carried for years and affect social development as the child moves into the adolescent and adult years resulting in a vicious cycle where the individual diagnosed with AS continues to see people as threatening and themselves as invaluable objects.

Theme Four: Family Stress

Families with a child diagnosed with AS have many difficult hurdles to overcome. Many parents of children diagnosed with AS carry a great deal of shame and guilt (Lozzi-Toscano, 2004) and feel lost and confused as they attempt to deal with their child's special parenting needs. Due to the social, emotional, educational, and relational hurdles that come with having a child diagnosed with AS, parents and family members are rejected due to not being seen as a "normal" family. Parents can put themselves in a sort of a "prison" by believing that their child diagnosed with AS will not be accepted or because of the fear of rejection, they will isolate themselves away from social gatherings.

Families must deal with the emotional inflexibility and fears of the child diagnosed with AS and the behavioral acting out that often accompanies the emotional inflexibility and fears. Family members are subjected to the incessant talking of a child or sibling diagnosed with AS who is talking about their favorite toy or movie and if they try and stop the child there could be a tantrum or disruption. Family members must deal with the ritualistic behavior of a child diagnosed with AS who exhibits obsessive-compulsive thinking and behaviors and the possible physical outburst that occurs if the ritual is disrupted. As a result, families of children diagnosed with AS are often plagued by stress and feelings of desperation as they try to cope with all the possible challenges.

I have worked with several families who have a mix of a child or children diagnosed with AS and sibling who are neurotypical. These families have great amounts of stress as the parent or parents attempt to meet the needs of the child or children diagnosed with AS, and attempt to meet the emotional, mental, and physical needs of the neurotypical children. I hear from siblings who are "tired" of the sibling or siblings diagnosed with AS and feel that the parents "favor" the sibling diagnosed with AS. One girl, spoke of her brother with a great deal of anger towards him, "We can't even go out to dinner anymore because of how he acts in the restaurant. It's pathetic. I never want to have my friends over because I am embarrassed." One mother shared her frustration in having a son diagnosed with AS and how her other two children "had normal lives with friends, activities, and futures" she said, fighting back tears, "I just worry so bad that he is being left behind, but I can't neglect his siblings!" As I mentioned earlier, I firmly believe that the families of children diagnosed with AS need coping skills to deal with the stress that comes from trying to be "normal" in a culture in which no one is "normal", yet tremendous pressure exists to force families into a specific mold.

Marital stress is another complication of having a child diagnosed with AS. Any couple with a special-needs child is going to feel the strain on their relationships as they try and focus on the needs of their child, themselves, and the relationship. Parents/caregivers of children with AS often appear to be in a state of "fight-or-flight" and share with me that they are "just trying to get through the day" and then flop into bed. There is little time for intimacy and each falls into a routine that increasingly tends to shut out their partner. Hartley, Barker, Seltzer, Floyd, Greenberg, Orsmond, and Bolt (2010) cite the potential for greater marital discord for couples that have a child on the autism spectrum. Their research points out the need for therapists working with these families to assist in strengthening the parent/caregiver unit through encouraging the couple to create special time for each other. While the demands on the relationship are great, the divorce rate is not as high as commonly reported in the popular media (Hartley, et al., 2010).

Chapter 5

Play Therapy Toys and Techniques with Children Diagnosed with Asperger's Syndrome

OVERVIEW

Play therapy has a very rich history and has been well documented in being an effective therapy approach with children and adolescents (Koocher and D'Angelo, 1992; Leblanc and Ritchie, 2001; Shaffer and Lazarus, 1952). Children diagnosed with AS typically show deficits in spontaneous and imaginative play (Lu, Peterson, Lacroix, and Rousseau, 2009), and incorporating this type of play into the therapy work can bring great benefits for the child. Using play therapy in my work has provided me with an amazing tool with which to help young people over the past 15 years. Some of the major theorists and practitioners that have impacted me on my journey of study and practice of play therapy include: Melanie Klein, Virginia Axline, Garry Landreth, Risë VanFleet, Dan LeGoff, Byron and Carol Norton, Charles Schaefer, and David Crenshaw. I recommend their work to anyone who is interested in broadening their skills and learning more about this amazing tool.

My play therapy approach with children and adolescents diagnosed with AS follows Schaefer's "prescriptive approach" (2001) in which toys and techniques are chosen based on the needs of the child and the problem presented. While at times I find non-directive play is useful in building a relationship with a child, I lean toward a directive approach when working with children and adolescents diagnosed with AS. This chapter connects toys and techniques with the themes discussed in Chapter Four and uses case examples throughout the chapter to demonstrate how the toys and techniques can be utilized.

TOYS AND TECHNIQUES TO HELP THE CHILD DIAGNOSED
WITH ASPERGER'S SYNDROME CONQUER FEAR

Puppets and Stuffed Animals

Bromfield (1989) demonstrated the use of puppets with a boy with high functioning autism who had many debilitating fears and I have found this very useful in both helping the child communicate information about their fears as well as use the perspective of another (the therapist's puppet) to help the child understand social surroundings. Puppet play can help relieve the child's anxiety because the child is in control of the situation, and is free to experiment with various elements of social situations. The therapist can use their puppet to bring up the fearful situation, or to verbalize how the child might be feeling. Then the child can voice feelings and thoughts through their puppet and provide feedback regarding fears in a safe way. Stuffed animals can also be used. The use of puppets and stuffed animals are also wonderful tools to begin working on emotion recognition and perspective taking.

I have used stuffed animals for children diagnosed with AS who have fears as a result of being bullied in school or in the neighborhood. For instance, the child designates a stuffed animal that represents themselves and then one that represents the bully, and picks other stuffed animals to represent other friends, classmates, or neighborhood children. Much like with the puppet play, the child can verbalize feelings and thoughts through the stuffed animal and look at the fear from a different perspective that is safe. The child can also play the role of the bully which can instill feelings of empowerment and get the child to practice perspective taking. The therapist is able to gather insight from the play to better understand what the child is thinking and feeling and model social skills by joining in the play.

Lego Play

LeGoff (2004) and Owens, Granader, Humphrey, and Baron-Cohen (2008) cite the use of Lego play to help build social skills in children with AS and state that children diagnosed with AS tend to be drawn to toys such as Lego sets "due to the fact that people with autism are particularly attracted to systems" (Owens, et al., p. 1945). I have found that children diagnosed with AS or who have AS traits have a strong interest in Lego sets, and I have used them in play therapy for many years. Lego sets are valuable therapy toys with children diagnosed with AS not only because of the system and structure characteristics, but the Lego figures that are part of the building sets allow the therapist to play out social situations with the child. The recent connection between Lego and Star Wars, Indiana Jones, and Harry Potter make Lego sets unique for use in the therapy room with children diagnosed with AS who often love these movies, and provide metaphors to use with children such as "the force" in Lego Star Wars or Indiana Jones' spirit to never give up even when it seems he has reached the end of "his rope."

When a child diagnosed with AS is dealing with a particular fear that relates to a social situation or a place (school, restaurant, etc.) it can be helpful to have the child build a structure using Lego bricks that represents that place or building. When the child is building the structure, it provides the child a sense of control and/or safety over the fear as they see the building in miniature form. I have used this technique with children diagnosed with AS who have school fears related to going into the classroom, lunchroom, or the building itself. Once the building is built, I will introduce Lego figures that the child can use to represent him or her and the various people in the school world. From that point, the child is allowed to play out any scenario they want and the therapist is available to interpret meaning from the play as well as work on emotion recognition and increase social skills to help alleviate the fear.

I used Lego sets with a second-grade boy diagnosed with AS who was struggling with school fears. I instructed him to build his school and to my surprise he also built a helicopter pad complete with a helicopter and pilot behind the school that he said would "fly him away" if he wanted it to. The boy created a Lego character that represented him and in the play his character would often leave the school and get in the helicopter and fly away. I used the helicopter as a metaphor for a special teacher that the school had provided that the boy could go to if he was feeling overwhelmed. Over the next several sessions, we were able to examine other fears that the boy had through playing with the miniature school made of Lego bricks. Over time, many of the boy's fears of school diminished and he told me that he felt safer at school.

Art

Art therapy has long since been recognized as a powerful tool in the playroom, however in recent years, studies have emerged examining the use of art with children diagnosed with AS (Epp, 2008; Evans and Dubowski, 2001; Lesinskiene, 2002). I have found that art is a wonderful medium to allow the child diagnosed with AS to express thoughts and ideas about their fears, as well as be exposed to learning coping skills to deal with their fears. One technique that works well with children diagnosed with AS is to present them with art materials (paints, markers, colored pencils, paper, clay, Play Doh, etc.) and to give them the opportunity to freely express themselves. This can lead to the child expressing blocked or unconscious fears through the opportunity to freely express themselves through drawing or painting (Lesinskiene, 2002).

One problem that arises with children diagnosed with AS is that the fear and anxiety that plagues them often manifests in an inability to create through the medium of art. In fact, I have encountered children diagnosed with AS who exhibit heightened anxiety when they are presented with a blank sheet of paper and go into "shutdown" mode, refusing to even pick up a pencil. One technique that I use in this situation is to get the child to talk about what they are afraid of (school, bullies, monsters, etc.) and I draw a representation of whatever that is. While I am not a gifted artist by any means, a quick sketch of the object suffices to get the child talking. And, in traditional Aspergian style, the child will usually let the therapist know if the drawing is not adequate or needs a special feature ("The monster's nose is *not* that big!").

One boy who came to me had a specific fear of monsters and was experiencing nightmares. His fear was triggered by any sort of mask, and even the characters at Disney (Pooh, Mickey, etc.) would trigger weeks of nightmares and refusal to leave the house. As you can imagine, Halloween was a dreaded experience for this little guy. I used this technique of drawing monsters to get him verbalizing about the fear. I made the monster a little fat at first with faces that looked almost funny, and then gradually made them more menacing as they no longer evoked a fear response. As I drew, I verbalized to the boy "This is just ink and paper; these faces I am making, they cannot hurt me. If I want to I can give him girly hair and lipstick (boy begins to giggle), or I can make him wearing a dress (boy is now fully laughing). Later, the boy joined me in making monsters and eventually we placed them around the room and shot them with rubber bands. Later, I held the pictures up and he punched some of them that resulted in ripping the paper. This was a constant theme in our therapy sessions, and after three months the fears of masks and monsters had almost completely disappeared.

Video Games

My dissertation work (Hull, 2009) involved demonstrating the use of video games as a play-therapy tool with children suffering from emotional problems. I found there was very little information on the use of video games in the traditional literature; however, there is an increase in the use of video games as a play-therapy tool. I believe that many traditional play therapists shy away from using video games because of how children, especially children diagnosed with AS with OCD tendencies, tend to perseverate on video or computer games, and the therapists believe that the child will shut down once they become involved in the game. I do not fault anyone for holding this belief, because when one observes children playing a video or computer game, it is easy to feel as though one could explode a bomb next to the child and the child would not budge. However, as someone who plays video games, I believe that video and computer games hold great value in the therapy realm and I have used them for over 10 years.

Using video games in therapy provides a way to bond with the child by getting into their world. I often am able to gain great insight into how a child diagnosed with AS thinks, feels, and relates to the world based on the video games they enjoy playing as well as observing how they play them. LeGoff (2004) and Attwood (1998) state that incorporating a child's stereotyped interests into the therapy realm can provide a natural motivation to engage in the therapy process rather than introducing something unfamiliar that may create barriers. I have found that many children diagnosed with AS have a natural affinity for computer game and video games.

The types of games that I recommend to use in play therapy with children diagnosed with AS are the ones that have a two-player option (Lego Star Wars, Lego Indiana Jones, Mario Brothers, Wii Sports, etc.) that allows the building of the therapeutic relationship and also models working together toward a goal. The characters in the games and the quests can become metaphors for real-life situations. For example, the "clones" from Lego Star Wars that constantly try to attack the player and thwart progress can be used to illustrate bullies. Challenges that have to be completed to get to the next level can be used as metaphors for conquering fears and getting through situations that the child diagnosed with AS views as unpleasant. When a metaphor presents itself, I push the pause button on the controller to stop the action to explain the metaphor.

For example, one boy diagnosed with AS had fears of the fire bell at school. Because of this fear he did not want to attend school and would spend each day anxiously waiting to see if it was a "fire drill" day. This daily anxiety began to wear on him and he began missing days of school at a time. At the second session, he and I were playing a video game which he enjoyed very much and I suddenly noticed that the action in the game had all sorts of blinking lights and various sounds; such as explosions, machinery, and blaring signals. I pressed the pause button on the game controller and pointed this out to him and asked what was different between the sights and sounds in the game and the "terrifying" fire alarm bell. He said that the fire alarm bell was unpredictable and that there really might be a fire in which "everyone could burn to death." I agreed with him, and I asked him what would happen if there really was a fire, to which he replied that the person who first noticed the fire would notify the office and the office would notify the fire department and everyone would go outside in an organized manner. I then asked what he had to do in the video game with his character to get through the level and survive. He said that there was an organized sequence of events that if followed his character was kept out of danger and the level was completed. "Isn't that a lot like the school fire drill system?" I asked. He agreed with me that it was. Through playing the game together and applying a concept from the game to a real-life fear, he was able to look at the situation and the fear from a different perspective. The boy's fear of the fire alarm bell soon diminished and his anxiety related to going to school was eradicated.

TOYS AND TECHNIQUES TO HELP THE CHILD DIAGNOSED WITH ASPERGER'S SYNDROME LEARN SOCIAL SKILLS AND DEAL WITH RELATIONAL DIFFICULTIES

As previously discussed, the individual diagnosed with AS misses important social cues and social learning opportunities due to the complications caused by joint attention deficits, mindblindness, and alexithymia. My belief in studying the research, reading firsthand accounts of adults who have written about the difficulties of living with AS, as well as working with children and adolescents in therapy is that the child or adolescent diagnosed with AS needs a "picture" to help understand the concepts that neurotypical individuals seem to naturally acquire. Once the child or adolescent has this "picture" of what the concept looks like it is easier for them to build a framework of thinking and behavior to help them incorporate socially acceptable behavior. The following play therapy techniques provide for the child a picture that then allows the child to learn the appropriate social response or behavior.

Roadmaps and City Streets

Building relationships is about connection. To build a relationship is to connect a physical body along with the mental and emotional parts to another body with its mental and emotional parts. In addition to these parts, there are components of the brain, mind, and will of each person involved in the connection which are all framed against the backdrop of the culture. The culture determines what is "appropriate" and "acceptable." Parts of the cultural backdrop shift and change, and some parts never change. To successfully navigate both building and sustaining a relationship, one must be able to meld all these parts as well as notice, understand, and react appropriately to the signs and signals of the other person. A person must also understand the cultural shifts and changes. I discussed in Chapter Three how difficult this is for the individual diagnosed with AS. To help a child diagnosed with AS better understand relationships and connection, there must be a picture to help the child see the "components" of what makes a relationship.

A wonderful play therapy tool to begin the socialization process with a child diagnosed with AS is what I call "Roadmaps and City Streets." The child drives toy vehicles to places on the maps following the streets. The idea is to get the child thinking about the sequence of events and how places and buildings are connected by the streets. There are rules of driving that must be followed along the way such as stop signs, yield signs, traffic lights, and so forth. The metaphor for this play therapy activity is to show how relationships and navigating social situations have the same components. This can be done with a large piece of paper that allows the therapist and child to draw streets or a play mat with streets already drawn on it that unfolds on the floor. Some advantages of making a map with the large piece of paper is it models social interaction because of the involvement of the therapist and child working together, and also allows the child to create a completely new map and draw the streets and landmarks that are familiar to them. I got this idea from the book *Dibs: In Search of Self* by Virginia Axline (1964) in which she describes her work with a young boy who was struggling with socialization and relationships. Her playroom contained a large play city complete with streets and buildings that helped lessen Dib's fears by instilling in him a sense of control by being in charge of "his" city. While she did not specifically focus on a play therapy technique since it was non-directive play therapy, the boy's fears were reduced and he began to explore and grow through playing with a map of the city.

I used this technique with a seven-year-old boy diagnosed with AS who was experiencing severe difficulties in relationships with family members and at school. I set up a large piece of paper with markers and together we drew city streets and put familiar landmarks such as his house, school, and church. The boy got several cars and trucks and began to put them on the map. We examined what streets had to be taken from his house to the bank, then to the church, etc. Using behavioral tracking I would comment as he played, "You have to follow the right streets to get where you want to go; you are following the traffic rules." He became very excited with this form of play and began to use blocks that represented other buildings and landmarks. He created an elaborate set of rules for his "city" that included stop signs, stop lights, and one-way streets. I then grabbed another large piece of paper and made streets on it, but in place of the landmarks I put the names of the members of his family, his teachers, and some classmates from school. Instead of stop signs and stop lights, I wrote in social rules like listening, waiting in line, and not hitting. He was puzzled but I explained this is a "social" map which has rules and sequences to follow just like a regular map. Using a toy car that represented me, I showed how I had to stop and listen if someone else was talking just like I had to stop if the sign said stop. I showed how if I was mad, I could never hit someone because that would be like speeding and would get me a ticket, or it would be like running over someone and hurting them, and then I would have to go to jail. The boy began to function much better in social situations and, because of this technique, a foundation of social rules and social understanding was laid.

Chess

While any board game can be used to model healthy social interaction because of the dynamic of the therapist and child playing together, I have found that chess has some extra components that work well to instill social understanding in children diagnosed with AS. First, chess has pieces that have a rank and power as well as rules for movement. Second, there is a board that represents a cultural or social backdrop on which the pieces move about and interact. Third, there is an organization and orderliness to the game that many children diagnosed with AS find appealing. When working with board games, students often ask me how to deal with a child who cheats or wants to change the rules, and I remind them that the purpose of the play is for the child to explore, establish safety, and work through their issues. Against this backdrop, rules have no meaning. Norton and Norton (1997) discuss the importance of "no rules" in play therapy. The child constructs rules based on their fulfillment needs and thus "cannot cheat" (p. 77).

   With the game of chess, a child may want to know "how" to play and then quickly re-organize the game to how the child wants it to be. I have experienced play sessions with children diagnosed with AS who have used the chess pieces as family members, classmates, or random human figures who migrate from the board across the floor and join a group of Lego Star Wars Storm Troopers who are attacking a medieval castle full of Beanie Babies. Much like the metaphor process used in the "Roadmaps and City Streets" technique, the "rules" of chess can be used to introduce the social rules and procedures that underlie relationships and social situations and lead the child diagnosed with AS to a greater understanding of how the social "game" works.

Stuffed Animals and Puppets

I discussed earlier how puppets and stuffed animals can be used in play therapy with children diagnosed with AS to help them conquer fears.

Stuffed animals and puppets can also be used to help the child learn appropriate social behavior as well as playing out social difficulties they are currently experiencing. For example, a boy diagnosed with AS was experiencing significant social problems in school and at home. I used Beanie Babies to represent some of his classmates and family members and constructed various social situations that he was struggling with. One particular situation that was creating a great deal of stress for himself and for his family was his compulsion to tell his family members "everything" about a topic that he found interesting. However, his explanation of a certain part of Star Wars could take forty-five minutes and when his family members or peers at school would simply walk away in a non-interested manner, he was not only confused by their behavior but then felt a sense of "pressure" that something was not "right" because he had not been able to completely finish telling them everything.

He picked a Beanie Baby to represent himself and I used a Beanie Baby to play the role of a peer or family member. Using this technique my Beanie Baby began to talk about NFL football, a topic that he thought was "stupid" and "*very* not interesting." However, when he wanted to talk about Star Wars, I kept on going and ignored him, talking incessantly about NFL football. His Beanie Baby began to jump up and down with frustration, but I kept mine going, but I was careful to monitor his frustration level which was beginning to rise. He then actually put his Beanie Baby down, walked over to a box of Lego bricks, and, and told me he did not want to play anymore. I gently brought him back to the Beanie Babies and we discussed his feelings during the exchange and he stated that he wanted to "get away" and felt "really mad" inside. I used this insight to show him how others might feel if they did not get to speak, and that when I kept talking he felt ignored and "mad" on the inside, and that might be how classmates and family members feel too. Suddenly, in one of the most amazing moments that I have experienced in play therapy with children diagnosed with AS, a lightbulb went off for this boy, and I watched with awe as his mind was able to see something from another's perspective for the first time. From this point, I was able to model conversation exchange with him in a game where my Beanie Baby was only allowed to say one thing about NFL football and his Beanie Baby only one thing about Star Wars. I rejoiced inside as he said to me, "I don't have to tell everything, right? I can just say one or two things and then stop, and I am allowed to tell you more later, right?" This play with the Beanie Babies was the picture for his mind in order to understand the social construct and make it real for him, whereas before he could not begin to grasp it. His parents and teachers stated they noticed a difference in his conversations with them and he had lessened his "obsessive talking" considerably.

Group Play

The benefits of group play have been increasingly recognized for children on the autism spectrum to help them acquire social skills (Epp, 2008; Neufeld and Wolfberg, 2010). Children diagnosed with AS tend to have deficits in social play (Lu et al., 2009), and researchers have found that group therapy settings help children diagnosed with AS by teaching them how to initiate social behavior and to practice joining with others in a social setting (LeGoff, 2004; Owens et al., 2008). I have found that group play therapy with children diagnosed with AS is useful in teaching social skills, forming connections between children with similar likes, struggles, and interests, and provides an environment to help children diagnosed with AS practice initiating social behavior. Group play therapy provides practice ground to incorporate the skills worked on during individual sessions such as perspective-taking, joint attention, and taking turns.

There are many different ways to conduct play therapy groups. I have found the work of LeGoff (2004) and Owens et al. (2008) helpful in utilizing various ways to incorporate group play therapy with children diagnosed with AS. One way is to have the entire group engage in an activity where all of the members are working together towards a common goal such as building a castle. A child gets to be the leader of the project and the rest are helpers, and then the roles of leaders and helpers are rotated so that each child gets to be "in charge." I divide the building project into sections and put a child in charge of each section. For instance, if the group goal is to build a castle, John will be the leader of building the turret and he will tell the rest of the group what pieces will be needed and how the turret will look. Phillip will be in charge of the cannons, and so on. The therapist's role in this exercise is to monitor that the "rules" of the group and the exercise are being followed. Rules are important in group work, and especially in working with children diagnosed with AS. Since the goal of the group play is to work on building socially appropriate behavior, the rules of the group can focus on social skills such as turn-taking, asking questions, using member's names to get attention, and so on.

Another way to utilize group play is to divide the group into smaller units of two or three members and use the same framework. I have found that the smaller groups are especially useful in the beginning of a group where new members can "warm up" instead of being thrown into a large group of children they do not know. Smaller groups also allow for focused attention from the therapist to identify turn-taking, gaze following, and joint attention. The children learn social skills in the small groups and those skills can be generalized to the larger group, which can generalize to other social groups outside of the therapy realm. The children can be rotated through the small groups by the therapist, so that by the end of the group therapy session each will have been with a different partner or partners.

There are many activities that can be used in the group play therapy sessions. Lego sets, Tinker Toys, Lincoln Logs, puzzles are just a few of the toys that can be used. I have a castle set that can be taken apart and put back together several different ways that I often use for group play therapy sessions. I also use video games in group play therapy sessions, where I utilize a two player game with themes of working together (Mario Brothers, Lego Star Wars, Lego Indiana Jones, and Lego Harry Potter). I pair the group members into groups of two and while two are playing the other group members watch and comment on the action. I have them rotate play either in 5 minute increments or at the end of each completed level. Through this play activity the group members work on social connection, taking turns, joint attention, and transitioning from play to observing roles.

TOYS AND TECHNIQUES TO HELP THE CHILD DIAGNOSED WITH AS EXPERIENCE AN INCREASE IN SELF-WORTH

I discussed in Chapter Four how low self-worth is a common theme in counseling for children diagnosed with AS and the devastating effect that low self-worth has in the lives of these extraordinary young people. Children diagnosed with AS often appear odd to peers and can be bullied and rejected, but inside each is a beautiful heart that can be wounded and carry scars just like any living thing. The toys and techniques presented here are designed to bring healing for the wounds of the children diagnosed with AS and to help them gain a sense of healthy self-worth.

Interests and Passions (Get in Their World!)

The first technique is not as much a technique as it is a way of getting into the child's world to see what makes them tick. I have always said that I have yet to meet two individuals diagnosed with AS who are exactly the same. It is important to find the interests and passions of the child diagnosed with AS because not only can this can help the therapist build rapport and trust with the child, but it can also provide valuable tools with which to bring into the play therapy realm and move the child toward growth. It is in our passions and interests, hobbies as they are sometimes called, that we find safety and serenity away from the hurried and frenetic pace of the outside world that demands so much of us. Children are no different, and especially those children diagnosed with AS who are frequent targets of bullying and social rejection. The interests and passions of these amazing children represent a "safe place," where the child can be in control and order their own private world, creating a realm that they alone understand and enjoy.

I have been awestruck when a truly miraculous phenomenon occurs in which a child or adolescent diagnosed with AS becomes my teacher as they allow me to walk through a door into their world. It may be learning about nature, possibly reptiles or birds, or showing me what insect makes those curious little cone shapes in the sand outside my office door. One boy showed me that right outside my office under the leaves of a scrubby little tree were hundreds of butterfly eggs. Butterfly eggs! I had no idea. It may be learning about Star Wars, or some distant planet that I have heard of, but never really knew. It may involve being taught how to play a video game with which I am unfamiliar. It may be a child teaching me about a Japanese anime T.V. show that appears to just be a cartoon on the screen, yet through watching it I find the very essence of wisdom for good living within the colorful frames. The power in this is that it not only lays a foundation for building the therapeutic alliance but also provides a boost to the child's sense of belonging and worth. Any time that a child gets to say to an adult "Let me show you!" a light begins to shine within the child that sends the message that "I have worth."

When the therapist is working with a child diagnosed with AS where low self-worth is a problem, remember to use words of encouragement and praise during the activity. A well-timed comment when playing a game ("Hey you did great on that level, I didn't know that door was there") or when building something ("I really like how you reinforced the wing so it is extra strong now, good job!") not only shows the therapist is interested and noticed what the child did, but gives the child the idea that something they did mattered.

"I am Unique" Technique

This technique involves helping the child diagnosed with AS see that they are a unique individual and that they are valuable. I discussed earlier the various barriers that children diagnosed with AS have in relation to seeing themselves and recognizing emotions and nonverbalized thoughts. This technique is designed to begin to lay a foundation of getting the child to notice themselves. As I begin playing with a child diagnosed with AS, I get them to talk about themselves and I keep a record on a notepad or whiteboard of their interests and activities they enjoy doing. If there is a specialty area, such as a child who loves nature but is particularly interested in reptiles, I write that down. I also write down special pets or special places they like to go. Using a large piece of paper, I have the child draw a picture that represents them and then together we write all of the items from the notepad or whiteboard. At the top of the paper I write their name with the words "I am Unique!" in big letters. We talk about what the word "unique" means and I emphasize the idea of celebrating the child's own talents, abilities, and interests, and that it is "o.k." to be different. The child can use markers, paints, or crayons to color their picture. The goal of this technique is to help the child see the special interests and abilities that make up who they are, and to build a pathway to increasing self-worth.

Building

This technique involves any toy that can be built, such as blocks, Lego bricks, Tinker Toys, or Lincoln Logs. The technique helps increase self-worth in two ways. First, the child is expressing themselves creatively and implies that something inside is being brought out. Building something requires the child to be able to see a picture in their mind, use their imagination, and then bring it to reality through putting the pieces together. This sequence represents a way to get the child to see that their interests and ideas are valuable. The second way that this technique helps in increasing self-worth is that the finished product represents something that the child has made thus making it valuable. By reinforcing this, the therapist can help the child see value and worth in what was created. The thought here is that if what was created came from inside the child and it is valuable, the child must be valuable as well. I recommend taking a picture of the creation as a way of preserving the memory of the creation. It also aids in sending a message to the child that it is valuable enough to be preserved through the photograph. I am often asked by children if I can "save" their creation and I tell them that I cannot guarantee that the creation will be there at the next session but that the opportunity to build something else will be. Norton and Norton (1997) address this issue and I agree with them. However, there are occasions where I have saved a creation to be added to later by the child because it had clinical significance in the course of therapy for that child.

Sand Play

Much like the building technique, sand play is an activity in which the child diagnosed with AS is given the opportunity to create in a spontaneous and imaginative way. More importantly, sand play can be an activity where the child creates his or her own "world" and can be in control of the world they have created. Sand play is recognized as a powerful tool in the play therapy world and much has been written about the positive effects of sand play

(Norton and Norton, 1997). New research is beginning to emerge regarding the positive effects of sand play with children diagnosed with autism. Lu et al., (2009) found that sand play helped to increase verbal expression as well as spontaneous and imaginative play, in addition to more engaged and sustained social interaction among the children diagnosed with autism. However, a caution of using sand should be noted when working with children diagnosed with AS in that, depending on their developmental level, the sand play can "stir up" intense emotion and the child may become overstimulated due to overwhelming emotional content that is baffling to them. When a therapist observes that a child is becoming frustrated, agitated, or begins to show "shutdown" behavior, it is best to gently guide them away from the sand to another activity.

I use sand play with children diagnosed with AS in order to encourage exploratory and imaginative play and also to increase the child's sense of self-worth. The theme in using sand play for self-worth is much like the building technique in that the therapist helps to get the child to connect the value in the sand creation and themselves. I have found that some children diagnosed with AS are not naturally drawn to the sand box. This may be due to the high numbers of children diagnosed with AS who have OCD tendencies and who do not like touching sand or dirt. Many children diagnosed with AS ask me if the sand is "dirty." I reassure them that the sand is washed and clean. The exploration of the sand box through sand play represents a metaphor for the child exploring thoughts and feelings.

I used sand play with a boy diagnosed with AS who suffered from low self-worth due to peer rejection and bullying. At first, he resisted playing in the sand box, sitting next to the sand but refusing to touch the sand or use any of the toys or tools presented to him. Knowing that he was interested in Star Wars, I placed some Star Wars figures in the sand and moved them around and he began to become engaged in what I was doing. He suggested that the smooth sand could be a "planet" that the figures landed on. He began to pull out various toys and objects to make "forts" for the figures. I told him that he was in charge and that I was his helper and instructed him to tell me what items he needed and that I could help build some of the structures if he needed me to. Suddenly, the boy's intensity began to bubble up from deep within. Gone was the fear of touching the sand. He was on a mission to construct a shelter for the Star Wars figures before the Clones came to attack. By the time he was finished, the boy had constructed a complex creation and he was beaming! While he was building, I cheered him on. "Great! This is amazing! That is a great idea to put a trap door there in case they need to escape!" When he was finished we took a picture of the creation. I continued to reinforce that the creation was valuable and that HE was valuable because of his ability to create it. For the next ten sessions, he only wanted to play in the sand with the Star Wars figures. Both his mother and teachers noted an increase in his self-worth, better social interaction with peers, and less anxiety in social situations.

Video Games

I discussed earlier how I have utilized video and computer games with children diagnosed with AS in conquering fear. Video and computer games can also be a path to increased self-worth in a child diagnosed with AS. When a child plays a game that is familiar and one that the child is skilled at playing, the therapist has an opportunity to capitalize on the feeling of accomplishment and satisfaction that accompanies the activity. I discussed earlier that many children diagnosed with AS are drawn to video games because the games represent a sequence and system of activity that the child can control. Many video and computer games contain themes of inner strength and require the player to focus on taking calculated risks to secure "health" or "one-ups" to continue through the game. These dynamics are easily relatable to the real-world experience of daily living in that one must be somewhat self-reliant and self-aware to achieve success in daily living. Herein is the essence of using video/computer games to help increase self-worth in children diagnosed with AS.

Building on the concept that self-worth is seeing oneself as valuable and worthy, the purpose of using of video/computer games with children diagnosed with AS is to help the child see that they have value and worth through not only the success that is achieved through playing the game but also through the elements of perseverance and internal strength found in the games. Perseverance and internal strength become metaphors for how the child views themselves. For instance, when a child's character "dies" or "fails" in the game he or she is playing, I have observed that most children will start over. Even if some disappointment or frustration is experienced, most children will continue on until the level is completed or the technique is mastered. To try again when one encounters failure requires inner strength that is made up of courage and determination. My dissertation work (Hull, 2009) demonstrated how video games were useful with children suffering from the emotional disturbance of sadness in raising their sense of self-worth.

I worked with a ten-year-old boy diagnosed with AS who suffered from low self-worth and who liked playing Lego Star Wars video games. One of the key elements of Star Wars is the concept of "the force," an internal power characterized by mental strength that is channeled from within and is manifested through physical power such as being able to jump very high and move very large objects. I use the concept of "the force" often as a metaphor with children in counseling relating to finding value in oneself, thinking positively, and making good choices. I began by getting the boy to tell me about "the force" and he excitedly shared about all of the powers that one can do when they have "the force," as well as the characters in the story that possess this special ability. "The force" became a metaphor for self-worth and as we played the game I was able to explain how powerful it is to think positively about oneself and to value one's abilities and interests. We wrote down all of the things that gave him value and labeled it "The Force." At each session, we talked about how he had used "The Force" since I had seen him last, and he was able to give me examples of ignoring mean comments, not reacting when he did not get his way, and even choosing to be nice to others. His teacher noted several new instances of empathy with classmates, and his mother noted that the self-hatred statements, that he had been making prior to beginning therapy, had ceased.

TOYS AND TECHNIQUES TO HELP PARENTS, CAREGIVERS, AND FAMILIES OF CHILDREN DIAGNOSED WITH AS

I discussed in Chapter Four how the families of children diagnosed with AS experience a great deal of stress. These families often struggle with acceptance of the difficulties of living with and caring for a child with AS and can experience shame and guilt (Lozzi-Toscano, 2004). When I work with a child diagnosed with AS, I meet with the parent(s) and/or caregiver(s) to assess the level of stress that is in the family unit. While my main focus of the therapy is the child, the family has a great deal of influence on the child. The child's emotional and psychological functioning can be impacted by the family, and without good coping skills the family may keep the child from developing properly. When stress gets too high and the family does not have good coping skills with which to deal with the stress, the family members may treat the child diagnosed with AS like a scapegoat. This scenario has the family blaming the child diagnosed with AS for every tiny problem encountered by the family. When the parental unit is solely focused on the child diagnosed with AS, the unit becomes stressed and can experience "separation, isolation, and frustration" (Lozzi-Toscano, 2004, p. 56). The intense focus on the child diagnosed with AS can lead to ignoring the needs of siblings and other members of the family.

I discussed the two extremes of parents/caregivers in Chapter Four: The "helicopter" overinvolved parent/caregiver and the under-involved parent/caregiver. The techniques discussed here are designed to move parents/caregivers toward the middle of those two extremes and to enhance the relationship between the child and the parents/caregivers. By doing so, the coping skills of the parents/caregivers to deal with stress increases and the door is opened for social skills modeling and healthy emotional development. Parents and extended family members play an important role in the emotional, psychological, and social development of the child diagnosed with AS. The therapist plays an important role in helping the parents/caregivers and family members better understand the child diagnosed with AS and to teach them valuable coping skills.

Play that Builds Connection

Playing together is a wonderful way to build connection between parents/caregivers and families and I use it often in my work. I am shocked by how many parents do not play with their children. When I explore this I find that many parents are either too busy or that play was not an important part of the parents/caregiver's development. Play is an interactive way for the parents/caregivers to get to know their child diagnosed with AS, and for the child to engage in exploratory play with the parent in a role-reversal: The child is the one in charge and leads the parent in play. I have combined two influential treatment approaches in this technique. The first is filial play therapy which is a process whereby the therapist teaches parents/caregivers to conduct play therapy sessions with the child in order to learn to identify themes in the child's play to help the child deal with difficulties and also create a more emotional bond with the child (VanFleet, 1994). The second treatment approach is one that has been developed by Stanley Greenspan and is known as Floortime (Greenspan and Wieder, (2007). Floortime is an interactive play technique between parents and children diagnosed with autism where the child leads the play and the parent is instructed to join in and be an active participant in the play. The goal is that through the intensive play sessions, the child's social and emotional development will be stimulated in addition to building a better bond with the parent/caregiver (Greenspan and Wieder, (2007).

The *Play the Builds Connection* technique is designed to have the parent join the child in play that utilizes the child's stereotyped interest. Much like Floortime, this technique puts the child in charge and forces the parent to follow the lead and join in the play. The benefit of this technique is that it helps lessen the control of the "helicopter" parent and builds independence in the child through the role reversal, while getting the under-involved parent into the child's world. Prior to utilizing this technique, I conduct two or three individual play sessions with the child to build a level of familiarity not only to learn what types of play the child likes, but to allow the child to be comfortable with my presence in the playroom. My role as the therapist in this technique is to model play behavior with the child so the parent/caregiver can see what it looks like to be joined with a child in play, as well as to instruct the parent on following the child's lead.

I used the technique with a single mother and her child diagnosed with AS. This mother vacillated between "helicopter" mode and the under-involved style. On one hand, she would overprotect and "baby" her son, letting her fears and insecurities dominate her parenting style; on the other, there was virtually no quality interactive time between them. When confronted with this observation she gave a common reply, "Well, he is just so into his Legos and that is all he wants to do, so I just do my thing." Yet, when I offered myself to play with the boy, he was more than eager to have a willing companion and proceeded immediately to "put me to work" in joining his play. I saw an opportunity to help lessen the controlling nature of the mother and help pull the boy up the developmental ladder through the *Play that Builds Connection* technique.

Her reaction was typical of most parents who are instructed to play with their children. "I don't know how to do this," "Gosh I haven't played in so long," "What am I supposed to do?" I gave her basic instructions at the beginning of the session and I am used to the initial resistance that parents often present. Most parents feel they might "do something wrong" and need the therapist to encourage them to "just be" and focus on connecting through play. I instructed the boy prior to bringing his mother into the session that he would be taking the lead and that his mother would be playing with him and she needed to know what to do. Using Lego bricks, the boy began to build a city and I instructed the mother to follow his lead. I prompted the boy to involve his mother in play by saying "Tell her what to do next," and I prompted the mother to ask him "What should I do now?" to get dialogue going between them. By the end of the session, both mother and son were dialoguing without any prompts and were connected in the play. This continued over six sessions, and I gave homework each week for mother and son to play together for at least 30 minutes per day. Through collaborative play the mother and son achieved a new level of connection. The mother was able to lessen her "helicoptering" and began to understand her son in a whole new way. The boy was able to become more independent and improved in his social skills at school.

Board Games

Board games provide a way to involve the whole family and build connection between parents, neurotypical siblings, and the child or children diagnosed with AS. I have used board games in therapy for a long time, not just with families who have a child or children diagnosed with AS. As someone who comes from a family-systems orientation, I find it interesting to watch a family playing Life or Monopoly together and seeing the various roles that each person takes on and observing the interactions between the members. Playing games has a way of bringing the best and worst out in people and I have observed that people tend to let their "guard" down when interacting with others in the close proximity that board games afford. Children diagnosed with AS tend to like board games because of the structure and rules that accompany them.

I discussed previously how families who have neurotypical children and a child or children diagnosed with AS often experience a great deal of stress in the family system and the child diagnosed with AS is often rejected by neurotypical siblings. The goals in playing board games with families who have a child or children diagnosed with AS are: 1) Build connection between family members that increases neurotypical family members' understanding of the child diagnosed with AS; and, 2) Provide socialization opportunities for the child diagnosed with AS. I have used games such as Trouble, Sorry!, and Uno in session because those games do not take as long as Life or Monopoly and fit well into the timeframe of a session. However, games like Life or Monopoly are good to prescribe as homework for the family to play outside of the office. My role as the therapist in utilizing board games is much like that in the *Play that Builds Connection* technique. I facilitate game play and share expectations for family members as well as the rationale for playing the game. I notice where connections can be made between family members and where stereotyped behaviors of the child diagnosed with AS can be "normalized" in order that these behaviors can be better understood by family members.

For example, I was using Uno with a family comprised of two parents, an eight-year-old boy diagnosed with AS and two neurotypical siblings. The neurotypical siblings (both older) were annoyed with the boy's behaviors and believed he got more attention from the parents than they did. When I investigated how much the parents had shared with the siblings regarding AS, I found that little had been shared with them. Like many families, the parents became reactive upon finding out the diagnosis and all the siblings knew was that mom or dad was not as available because their younger brother needed "a lot of help." The parents shared there had been little or no compromising among the three and that the two neurotypical siblings would often "gang up" on their brother diagnosed with AS. I observed this firsthand when the UNO® game began. The boy diagnosed with AS would constantly straighten the pile of lay-down cards during the game, which greatly annoyed the siblings. In the game of Uno the lay-down pile is notoriously unkempt as players are quickly laying down cards, and the boy's straightening of the cards after each player laid one down caused an interruption in the flow of the game. The two siblings reacted with frustration and anger and commented "You are so annoying!" "Why do you have to mess everything up?"

I allowed this to go on for a few moments and to watch how the parents would handle the situation. Both passively tried to get the siblings to stop, but to no avail. I called a "timeout" and with the action frozen I isolated the action of the boy diagnosed with AS straightening the lay-down pile. I asked him to talk about why he felt he needed to constantly straighten the pile. The boy was able to share that the cards seemed "out of line" and that it made him feel nervous that something bad might happen if the pile was not straightened. As I discussed earlier, many children diagnosed with AS exhibit OCD tendencies, which frustrate parents, caregivers, and family members. I asked the rest of the family members if they knew the reason for the boy's behavior and all of them indicated that this was new information to them. Using this new information as a foundation, I was able to help the family understand the reason behind the boy's behavior which helped to increase connection and empathy. Through these family play sessions, the family members were able to learn a skill of looking past surface behaviors to a more meaningful explanation of the boy's behaviors. Thus, the boy appeared less "annoying" to the siblings and new opportunities arose for connection between themselves and their brother. The parents were less frustrated with the boy's behaviors and were able to learn better techniques for dealing with difficult situations instead of lashing out or shutting down.

Family Art Projects

I discussed earlier how art can be used in the individual session with children diagnosed with AS. The use of art in family sessions is also a wonderful way to build connection between family members (Kerr, Hoshino, Sutherland, Parashak, and McCarley, 2008). The use of art is similar to the use of games, but instead of the family playing a game, the family as a whole unit constructs an art project. The goal is to bring the family together and to enhance connection, by building understanding and modeling important social and relationship skills for the child diagnosed with AS. The family can be given clay or other building material to construct a sculpture. Painting or coloring a picture together is another technique that can be used. The therapist's role is much like that in the game playing technique, serving as a director and facilitator in the activity and looking for opportunities to help build connection.

A CASE STUDY

The Case of Brian: Play Therapy with a Child Diagnosed with Asperger's Syndrome

Brian presented at my counseling office as an eight-year-old Caucasian male who was diagnosed with AS about six months prior. I had met with Brian's parents before meeting with Brian and they shared that he was having significant anxieties and fears related to social situations and adapting to change when the expected "normal" routine was not followed. Brian had developed significant temper tantrums, hand flapping, and OCD-type behaviors that had begun to become more frequent. Brian had a high IQ and was not having academic problems, but he had begun to give his parents significant problems in the morning getting ready for school and was having tantrums getting out of the car and going into the classroom. In school, Brian had become more difficult in the classroom. For instance, if he found he had missed one of his spelling words on a spelling test, he would throw himself on the floor and wail loudly, crying and crumpling up his paper. Brian's parents reported that his anxiety had become so intense when going to restaurants that they stopped going altogether. His mother stated that if she altered the afternoon routine after picking him up from school he would have a "meltdown" in the car, resulting in crying, screaming, and physically attacking her seat with punches and kicks. Brian's parents revealed that they had become so exhausted from these encounters with Brian that they no longer did any activities with him unless it involved tasks that had to be completed like homework or getting ready for bed. Brian had been started on an anti-anxiety medication two months prior to my meeting him and the psychiatrist had recommended therapy. Brian's parents reported noticing a lessening of the anxiety in the morning preparing for school, but that the tantrums continued as before.

Brian was very cautious when meeting me for the first time and stayed very close to his mother. I spoke slowly and told him the "rules" of the playroom, and encouraged him to explore. I sat on the floor in front of him and his mother and pulled out several large boxes of Lego pieces and placed them where he could see them. I also had a small toy train set that I pulled out as well. Brian's parents told me that he liked to play with Lego sets and mechanical toys like trains. He soon became interested and gradually moved to the floor with me. He soon became engrossed in play with the Lego bricks and the small toy train. He stated that he wanted to build a "bridge" that went over the train track, so that the train could go under it. I handed him various pieces and soon we were working together. Because I had previously inquired about Brian's interests, I was ready to offer him some toys that aligned with his stereotyped interests.

Lego play and the train set remained a constant for several sessions as I got to know Brian. I discovered that Brian also enjoyed video games and board games. Trust was built quickly with Brian, which I took as a very positive sign. The main treatment goal in my work with Brian was to alleviate the extreme anxiety that was plaguing him, in order to reduce the emotional and behavioral outbursts. Two of the main "triggers" of anxiety for Brian were social situations and a change in the expected routine. These fears relate to themes of safety and being in control. After a few sessions, I instructed Brian to build his school using Lego bricks to explore the issues surrounding school. During a few sessions using this play, it was revealed that Brian did not like large groups of people and said that they were "scary."

Using this information, in one session I used stuffed animals to represent a group and he picked out a stuffed animal that represented himself and he said that it felt like they were all "looking at me." At this point in the play, I spent several sessions using Lego people to play out social scenarios such as school, eating at restaurants, and going to church. In these sessions I had Brian role-play other roles through the Lego characters such as being the teacher, a classmate, or the server at the restaurant. He enjoyed this very much and I asked him if it felt "scary" to play these other roles and he said "no." I asked him about when he pretended to be the teacher and all those students were looking at him if that was "scary." He said "no" because "the teacher is doing her job and you have to look at the teacher." From here I was able to help Brian see that people look at other people not to hurt them, but because they exist and we use our eyes to see others so as to not bump into them, etc. Brian's parents noted a continued lessening of anxiety in social situations and his teacher reported a significant decrease in classroom outbursts.

I used video games to increase Brian's ability to tolerate unexpected change. One of his favorite games was Lego Indiana Jones, in which the main character has to navigate all sorts of unexpected threats and surprises to complete the level. Each level contains themes of danger and booby traps that thwart the player from reaching their goals. This provided a powerful metaphor to help Brian see that life is full of surprises and while his Mom is a very powerful character who usually accomplishes things in a predictable manner, sometimes the ground shakes, spears fall out of the sky, and thousands of snakes come out of nowhere and the plan has to be changed just like in Lego Indiana Jones. This was a fun way to help Brian see things from a different perspective and we were able to work on coping "tools" that Brian could use when he was feeling frustrated. Much like Indiana Jones' rope, Brian could imagine getting home a different way even though it was not the route he had expected his mother to take. Much like Indiana Jones' colleagues had tools like special books or wrenches to fix broken machinery, Brian learned that he could relax and remind himself that he was safe, even though the situation was not one that he had expected.

In addition to my individual work with Brian, I worked with his parents on being non-reactive and taught them parenting techniques to use to handle temper tantrums and outbursts. I taught them how to play with Brian and to allow him to lead them in play. Each week Brian's parents were given a homework assignment of playing with Brian and connecting with him. Over the next three months Brian's tantrums and outbursts became less frequent at home and the relationship with his parents became closer with the significant increase in quality time. Brian's parents reported feeling more connected with him and, instead of viewing AS from an outsider's vantage point, they said they began to understand Brian better as they were able to see life "through Brian's eyes."

The case of Brian is an example of how several different mediums of play were used to get to the root of what made Brian afraid in social situations. This case also demonstrates how parents can benefit from parenting techniques and how deeper connection and understanding of the child diagnosed with AS can be achieved through coaching. This process took over a year from start to finish and required a great deal of patience and commitment from Brian's parents. At times, I too struggled with patience as I wanted to "hurry" and get to a root cause and then find a solution. However, rushing and pushing Brian when he was not ready to reveal his fears would only have put unnecessary pressure on him and hampered therapeutic progress. This process also laid an important foundation for work that came later as Brian transitioned into the adolescent years. Because a relationship was already established, it was easy for Brian to re-enter therapy for work that needed to be done as he experienced emotional, mental, physical, and spiritual growth.

Chapter 6

Creating Connection and Examination of Themes in Play Therapy with Adolescents Diagnosed with Asperger's Syndrome

OVERVIEW

A common topic that arises among my students when I teach a class about conducting therapy with adolescents is getting adolescents to talk in therapy sessions. When I am asked this, I inquire back to the students "What makes you think that adolescents don't want to talk in therapy?" Most of my students have not yet worked with an adolescent in actual one-on-one therapy settings, but are simply voicing what they have heard. This is a good example of how adolescents tend to be victims of negative cultural stereotypes. For instance, a common cultural misconception is that adolescents do not value relationships with parents, yet research shows that adolescents do value relationships with parents and over half of adolescents surveyed in a recent poll identified at least one of their parents as a "hero" (MTV/Associated Press, 2007). I share with my students that I find the adolescents that I work with want to speak, but they often do not feel that the environments they share with adults are safe enough to share what is on their minds and hearts. Many of the adults, including therapists that adolescents encounter often do not listen effectively and talk at them instead of creating a partnership with them (Edgette, 2006).

Many people have the same misconception regarding adolescents diagnosed with AS who are referred for therapy. However, more and more research reveals that not only do adolescents diagnosed with AS want relationships with others, but that these adolescents do like to talk in therapy (Bromfield, 2010). Building connection with adolescents diagnosed with AS requires a therapist to be patient and willing to set aside personal agendas regarding therapeutic progress and traditional ideas about building rapport. Building the therapeutic relationship with adolescents diagnosed with AS requires the therapist to totally immerse themselves in the young person's world without pretense, judgment, or sarcasm. Like others who work with these amazing young people, I have found that an adolescent diagnosed with AS is very keen at recognizing patronizing behavior and fakeness.

I will never forget one young man who, with tears in his eyes, told me that he did not feel like I *really* cared for him. I was stunned by his reaction and comment because in my mind I was working very hard to build the relationship, and he sat stone-faced with no affect at all for three sessions saying very little. In a moment of brilliant honesty, he told me that he felt like he did with other adults who had worked with him in the past (teachers, tutors, etc.) that I was just "going through the motions." After praising his honesty, I first apologized and shared with him that I really did want to connect with him, and explained that the foundation of the work that I did with young people like himself was based on relationships. Then, I used his disclosure as a way to better understand his needs and wants, inviting him to openly say anything that he wanted to. I was stunned as he shared with me that he was very lonely and believed that he was not "good enough" to be noticed by people. It brought tears to my eyes as I realized that I had been working "very hard" to connect with him, but that was exactly the problem. In my "working hard" I appeared to be calloused and cold to him, yet because I was not getting any responses from him, I judged myself to be ineffective and needed to "work harder." I am so grateful for this young man's revelation to me! This encounter was a significant turning point in working with adolescents diagnosed with AS that led me to creating partnerships with them and learning from each adolescent instead of assuming that I knew their needs.

Creating connection with an adolescent diagnosed with AS requires the therapist to be willing to enter the teen's world and get to know the individual stereotyped interest of the teen. These interests may range from sports to nature and from video games to comic books. It is my belief that true connection requires more from the therapist than a passive interest during the session. Instead, true connection comes from immersing oneself into the interest of the adolescent whatever that may be. When a therapist shows genuine attentiveness to the interests of an adolescent diagnosed with AS, the therapist is communicating to the adolescent "I care about you," "You matter to me," and "You have value and worth." I have found that making myself knowledgeable about those things that the adolescent is interested in opens a door for the adolescent diagnosed with AS and they are usually surprised that an adult would want to know about the world that the adolescent is passionate about. To fully connect with the young people I have worked with over the years I began watching professional wrestling, checking out unique websites, began watching various Japanese anime television shows, began playing several video games, and listening to different types of music all because those things mattered to these amazing young people.

I found when I immersed myself in the various interests of the adolescents diagnosed with AS, amazing things began to happen in the sessions. The first change that I noticed was that a common bond began to form between myself and the teen, and the adolescent often showed surprise as I commented on the most recent episode of a TV show they liked or quoted some lyrics from a favorite song. In any relationship, shared interest fuels communication and connection. This "common bond" bridges people together and creates a unified passion for the interest as well as between the two people in the relationship. Another change I began to notice was that the adolescents often expressed a heightened interest in coming to the sessions and began to be more vocal and animated. For a lot of the teens, they experienced a new phenomenon of being an "instructor" of an adult (me) by teaching me about their interest, which created excitement and opportunity. This "role-reversal" opened the door for future work on perspective-taking and modeling of joint attention and social skill building. Perhaps one of the greatest changes I noticed by incorporating this into my work with adolescents diagnosed with AS was the creation of respect. As I came to better understand the adolescent through immersing myself into their select interest, I came to a new-found respect for them by learning new intricacies of how they saw the world and learning what made them "tick." I also found the adolescents respected me because of the time that I had invested in learning about their interest, and when I would converse with them about the topic there was a deepening of the connection between us.

Finally, by immersing myself into a new world, I began to adopt new thinking patterns by seeing the world through the eyes of the adolescents diagnosed with AS. I began to find what "excitement" meant to them; what "humor" meant to them; what "anger" meant to them; what "love" meant to them. It was as if I was putting on "Asperger" goggles and walking, feeling, smelling, and touching life as the young person did. My world got bigger and expanded; my therapeutic senses became sharpened and I began to grow in new ways. This was instrumental in not only connection on the surface of interests, but allowed a deepening of exploration into caverns of emotions and thinking. As I did this, I also noticed the deepening of trust that laid an important foundation for later work with the adolescent on topics such as hygiene, social skills, and discussions of sensitive topics like sexual feelings and relationships.

One young man who came to therapy was very interested in a Japanese anime TV show and wanted to bring his collection of DVDs of the series which contained four seasons of shows. Because there were no commercial interruptions, the episodes were about 22 minutes long. I have found that for children and adolescents diagnosed with AS in particular, the offering to share their stereotyped interest with another person, especially an adult is their way of saying "I like you" and "I trust you." I agreed and we began watching an episode every other session and then would discuss the material in the show. I am someone who constantly looks for metaphor in any material that I am using with young people whatever their interest may be. I was amazed by this show as the episodes contained themes of family, loss, love, relationships, courage, fear, humor, and friendship. I soon found this was much more than a cartoon; the material was rich and deep. I must admit that it was hard at times to not get the series for myself to see what was going to happen, but the young man made me promise to not look ahead but to wait for our sessions to watch the story unfold. This experience took well over a year but the rewards have been amazing! Through the themes of the show, I was able to tie concepts together and discuss issues using the characters in the show as reference points. Suddenly, I had "material" to work on the common deficits of AS like mindblindness, alexithymia, and lack of joint attention. Because of the young man being familiar with the show, he was able to grasp concepts for the "real world" from the metaphors present in the show. The themes of courage and bravery as well as dealing with the unexpected were very useful as this young man transitioned through various life stages.

I am a strong proponent of sharing this philosophy with the parent/caregivers of the adolescent diagnosed with AS so they can understand the importance of connecting with adolescents in this manner. As discussed earlier, parents and caregivers who understand and support the process of therapy become advocates and are more willing to modify their behaviors and accept greater responsibility. This process of connection is also a way to model connection for parents who feel like outsiders when it comes to the interests of their teen. I occasionally encounter a parent that questions the validity of listening to a teen's music or playing a video game during a session. I use this questioning as a way to educate and to explain the importance of connection through the stereotyped interests of the child and share research that supports the effectiveness of using an already established stereotyped interest in the therapy sessions (Attwood, 1998; LeGoff, 2004). Most importantly, I want to build trust with the parent and help them learn to be patient with the process. Parents want results and want to know that they are investing in something that works, but they need to know that while some gains may be made quickly, others take more time. Through helping the parent understand the importance of establishing connection, the therapist creates a connection of trust and communication with the parent that leads to parental advocacy for the adolescent diagnosed with AS.

CREATING COMMUNICATION FLOW WITH ADOLESCENTS DIAGNOSED WITH AS

Creating communication flow is important in therapy with adolescents diagnosed with AS. By "communication flow" I mean there is dialogue passing from the therapist to the adolescent and back again. However, communication flow does not mean there has to be filling of every minute with talking. I have had several adolescents and some adults diagnosed with AS tell me that a barrage of questions overwhelms them and I have observed that many will shut down and simply sit without responding when this happens. This is especially prevalent in the early stages of therapy when the therapist is "digging" for detailed information and the adolescent is still wondering if it is safe or not to share what is on their heart and mind. Our culture relies heavily on verbal interaction to form relationships and verbal exchange is highly valued. For those who are not adept at verbal exchange, every interaction can be excruciatingly uncomfortable. However, verbal exchange is not the only form of communication and the therapist that is going to work with adolescents diagnosed with AS must be comfortable with silence.

Early on when I began working with adolescents diagnosed with AS, I did not understand this and made this mistake. Once again, one young man was very gracious and directly told me that I was "very annoying" to talk to and that he felt frustrated with me. He finally said, "You ask too many questions! Give me time to answer!" and after I apologized profusely (it is a wonder that he ended up trusting me at all!) we were able to use his frustration to connect on a deeper level. He explained how he felt overwhelmed when he was asked too many questions, especially questions that were vague. He said that when he was asked a question, his brain took in every word, and then analyzed every possible response. So if I asked him a question such as, "Was it a good weekend with your Dad?" his brain would do something like this:

What does good mean?
What did I do with my Dad?
I ate four meals with my Dad, we went to three different places, and we watched two movies. (His brain would then go back and analyze each place and each interaction and in this case, each movie).
What do I need to tell that would make it "good?"
How much should I say about each thing?
What if I start talking and I am interrupted and can't finish?

He explained further that he analyzed *every* possible response, which was a major factor in appearing as though he was ignoring me, yet his brain was performing these amazing calculations and evaluations. When he would pause and not answer and stare out the window, I would either modify my question or fire another. I cringe even now as I write this when I think of how I overwhelmed his brain! Suddenly, however, as he explained this to me it hit me how important this was! My initial blunder proved helpful in getting to this new level of understanding. Bromfield (2010) brilliantly discusses this element of repairing a relationship when there is a misunderstanding between therapist and client and building a relationship through the modeling of empathy as well as the therapist offering apologies and making amends. These themes definitely were important during this phase of working with this young man. This young man's ability to communicate was also hampered by an internal compulsion to share *everything* that related to the event in question. Through better understanding of how his brain worked, we were able to isolate that part of his thinking process and gradually he became able to modify it and control it. A final benefit to understanding this element of this young man's thinking process was explaining to his family members how they could better communicate with him. Further, this knowledge helped to reframe instances in the past where he had simply shut down in places like school or church functions when neurotypical individuals would force questions upon him.

This exchange led to a better understanding of the value of silence and patience in speaking with individuals diagnosed with AS. This experience also changed my interviewing skills with neurotypical individuals who did not struggle with the challenges of AS. This has been one of the most valuable experiences in my work with young people diagnosed with AS and was a reminder to me of how important it is to throw out the agenda of my definition of progress and simply focus on connection and seeking to understand the amazing person sitting before me. I have compiled some techniques that can help encourage the flow of communication between a therapist and an adolescent diagnosed with AS.

Patience in Questioning

Therapists need information. Without it we are lost and cannot understand our clients nor can we know what the client wants and needs to help them achieve their treatment goals. Most neurotypical individuals communicate quite easily and information flows in an organized manner between therapist and client. The therapist is able to gather large amounts of information in a short amount of time. Most therapists are trained in interviewing skills that elicit large amounts of information and in this age of managed care and solution-focused approaches these skills are valuable. Enter the world of Asperger's and everything is different! Questions are met with silence; and answers are short and limited to one or two words when a response is given. A therapist often gets to the end of the session with only surface information and can feel as though the entire session was a waste. Much like my experience with the young man I discussed earlier, a therapist may feel led to begin firing more and more questions, which can lead to the shutdown of the adolescent diagnosed with AS and an increase of self-doubt and frustration in the therapist.

Patience in questioning is a key component of the initial interview process with adolescents diagnosed with AS. The therapist must remember the difficulty that individuals diagnosed with AS have in regards to social interaction, particularly verbal exchanges. As Weber (2008) notes:

> Most individuals with Asperger's syndrome have pervasive deficits in their understanding of what is communicated to them through the use of words and the flow of nonverbal information communicated. The deficits are noted in their understanding of and presentation in tone, rhythm, inflection of voice, body language, facial expression, and gaze modulation. These deficits lead to an overly literal interpretation of metaphors and images, and an incomplete understanding of oral communication that is insufficiently explicit. (p. 16)

Patience in questioning the adolescent diagnosed with AS means speaking slowly and clearly. It means framing questions in a simple and clear manner, avoiding vague references. The therapist must never assume that the child, adolescent, or adult diagnosed with AS understands references common to neurotypical individuals and innuendo that neurotypical individuals often use. Patience in questioning also means that the therapist accepts the information that the adolescent provides and resists the urge to "dig" when it is clear that the adolescent does not want to further discuss a topic.

Become Comfortable with Silence

I have observed that most people I meet are uncomfortable with silence. I conduct an exercise in my therapy classes with my students where I ask them if they are comfortable with silence and ninety percent of them dutifully shake their heads yes. I then stop speaking and just gaze at them. It only takes about ten seconds for the squirming to begin, then a giggle, then an outburst of frustration. Barely a minute goes by and someone usually yells out, "Okay, we get the point!" I do this with my students to show them that most of them really are not comfortable with silence. Silence in the therapy process is very powerful; but we have been conditioned to fill every space with noise, from TV to talking on the phone or listening to an iPod. Working with individuals diagnosed with AS requires the therapist to be comfortable with silence. While many adolescents diagnosed with AS are very verbal, many are not. As I demonstrated in the example earlier in the chapter, becoming comfortable with silence was a key component in the young man speaking and opening up to me.

Learn Their Language

I often tell people that I have never met two individuals diagnosed with AS who share the same characteristics. The way that an individual diagnosed with AS communicates, thinks, plays, and relates to others is completely unique. So too are the ways in which the individual diagnosed with AS shares information. I have found that teens, whether diagnosed with AS or neurotypical, tend to value individuality and have their own language. Adolescents diagnosed with AS share information in their own way, at their own pace, and with their own metaphors. It is important that the therapist working with an adolescent diagnosed with AS pay close attention to the ways in which the individual adolescent shares information and receives information. Once the therapist learns the way the adolescent communicates, a foundation is laid for the relationship to go to a deeper level which leads to deeper exploration in the "working" stages of therapy. Valuable information is derived from both verbal and non-verbal exchanges during this process.

For example, one young man diagnosed with AS that I worked with never stuttered until he began to discuss emotional-laden content. I realized this after a few sessions when I stayed silent for some time after asking him a question. I noticed after several exchanges that he quickly gave me a "surface" answer that was very short each time I asked him a question. I found if I waited, he would elaborate and would appear to become uncomfortable and start to stutter. This was very valuable because it alerted me to the fact we were in emotional territory, which caused him discomfort that led to the stuttering. Because there was a good therapeutic relationship established, I was able to inquire about the stuttering which led us into exploring the emotional content and eventually getting to the root of why the emotional material made him uncomfortable.

THEMES IN PLAY THERAPY WITH ADOLESCENTS DIAGNOSED WITH ASPERGER'S SYNDROME

I wrote in Chapter Four that the themes presented were not an exhaustive list, and the same principle applies in this chapter. The themes that I am presenting are ones that I have encountered in everyday practice as well as those that are commonly discussed in the literature. I think it is important to remember that each adolescent diagnosed with AS is unique, complete with their own way of seeing the world as well as possessing exceptional interests, gifts, and talents. I have included a section on working with families of adolescents diagnosed with AS because I am a firm believer in the family being a key component in the young person's development. Parents/caregivers of adolescents diagnosed with AS can experience increased levels of stress as developmental changes such as puberty and transitional components such as moving from middle school to high school often intersect, creating mental and emotional upheaval in the adolescent diagnosed with AS. Chapter Seven will discuss the application of play therapy toys and techniques for each theme discussed here.

Theme One: Low Self-Worth

Adolescents in general tend to struggle with low self-worth, regardless of whether they are diagnosed with AS or neurotypical. Low self-worth appears to be some of the emotional residue that accumulates as the young person struggles with identity formation and breaking away from the family unit. New social pressures, as well as the increased need for acceptance from family and peers, combine to create a choppy sea of insecurity and self-doubt. The adolescent diagnosed with AS is not immune to these rough waters. Therapists who work with adolescents diagnosed with AS know that this time of life is just as turbulent if not more so for the adolescent who lives with the challenges of AS. A common myth is that the adolescent diagnosed with AS does not feel the same social, emotional, or mental pressure that a neurotypical adolescent does; however, new research in the professional community and personal accounts of those living with AS prove otherwise. A wonderful book that helps delve into the mind of the adolescent diagnosed with AS is written by Luke Jackson. Luke, a thirteen-year-old adolescent diagnosed with AS writes with candor and clarity regarding life as an adolescent diagnosed with AS complete with the struggles and trials that living with AS brings (Jackson, 2002). One of the amazing parts of his personal account is the desire to fit in but living with AS causes him to appear to be very different. As he continues to learn about himself and how to interact with others, Luke finds ways to adapt and successfully navigate the world and through struggle creates inner strengths (Jackson, 2002).

I wish that all adolescents diagnosed with AS could have resilience like Luke, however, many do not. Adolescence is a time that places all adolescents at risk for suicide and depression, and the risk of depression and suicide for adolescents diagnosed with AS is also a reality (Wing, 1981), partly due to adolescence being a time when social relationships play an important role (Barnhill, 2001). Adolescents diagnosed with AS suffer from low self-worth due to a myriad of reasons. The main reason appears to be associated with the social and relational difficulties that leave the adolescent feeling isolated and rejected (Carter, 2009), which leads to feelings of loneliness that are carried into adulthood (Baron-Cohen, 2000). Barnhill (2001) demonstrated how adolescents diagnosed with AS tend to attribute social and relationship difficulties to their ability, which increased their risk for depression. Ghaziuddin, Ghaziuddin, and Greden (2002) found that high functioning autistic individuals with normal intelligence tended to view themselves as less competent, which increased feelings of low self-worth, and the more socially inept the person became the more negatively they viewed themselves.

Another factor that leads to feelings of low self-worth in the adolescent diagnosed with AS is depression. Research reveals that rates of depression tend to increase as the individual diagnosed with AS gets older, and those diagnosed with AS seem to be more prone to low self-worth and depression (Ghaziuddin et al., 2002). Many adolescents diagnosed with AS that are referred to me report experiencing periods of depression and many researchers speculate that this may be due to the difficulty that the adolescent diagnosed with AS has expressing feelings, particularly sadness (Barnhill, 2001). One young man diagnosed with AS was referred to me following his discharge from the psychiatric ward of a local hospital for a suicide attempt. He described his struggle with depressed feelings stating that it felt like he "was being swallowed up by an invisible force" and when this happened there was nothing he could do to "make it stop." When I inquired about the factors that led to his depressed episode, he stated that he could not pinpoint any event that could have triggered the depression. He only said that "I just had been feeling really sad for a long time." He further elaborated that his feelings of depression were very "confusing" to him; which supports the literature regarding individuals diagnosed with AS who struggle with alexithymia. Over time this young man attributed his feelings of depression to the thought that he had done something wrong which resulted in very low self-worth. A study by Shtayermman (2008) of adolescents and young adults diagnosed with AS revealed that a high percentage of adolescents and young adults diagnosed with AS reported clinically significant rates of suicidal thinking, depression, and anxiety.

A final factor that leads to low self-worth is social rejection and bullying that I will address fully in another section to follow. Adolescents diagnosed with AS look different, sound, different, and communicate differently from peers. These differences lead to the adolescent diagnosed with AS being seen as different. Adolescence is a time of striving for acceptance and connection with peers, and many times the social pecking order has no tolerance for someone with even the slightest unique characteristic. When an individual continues to be rejected, it is normal for the person to begin to believe that they are flawed and damaged. For young people diagnosed with AS who are struggling through the turbulent waters of adolescence, ridicule and rejection lead to patterns of negative, irrational thinking that ultimately result in low self-worth. What saddens me the most is that individuals diagnosed with AS are some of the most dynamic and interesting and brilliant individuals I have ever met. The conglomeration of talents, gifts, knowledge, and a completely unique perspective of the world leave an indelible impression that one has been in the presence of greatness. Yet, most of the adolescents diagnosed with AS do not see themselves that way, and the time of adolescence is a time of great risk for damage to be done to their fragile sense of self.

Theme Two: Bullying and Social Rejection

I have written extensively on the effects of bullying and social rejection previously when I discussed how bullying and social rejection affects children diagnosed with AS. However, I feel that it is necessary to discuss it in this section regarding adolescents diagnosed with AS because of how pervasive bullying and social rejection is for any adolescent who does not fit into the expected social norms, not just those diagnosed with AS. I have found that there are two key characteristics of adolescents diagnosed with AS that make them vulnerable to the onslaught of internal and emotional damage from bullying and social rejection. The first characteristic relates to mindblindness, and the second relates to alexithymia.

I discussed in Chapter Three that mindblindness is a term that describes the inability of the person diagnosed with AS to foresee and understand the intentions of others (Baron-Cohen, 1995). As the child diagnosed with AS transitions into adolescence, mindblindness continues to cause problems in building and sustaining relationships. Mindblindness interrupts the ability of the adolescent diagnosed with AS from distinguishing behaviors as friendly and playful, or threatening and dangerous. For example, I worked with a young man diagnosed with AS who played for his high school's baseball team. One afternoon I got a call from the young man's father who requested an emergency session and stated that something had happened in the locker room after practice and that the young man was not hurt, but that he desperately wanted to talk with me. Fearing the worst, I arranged the appointment. As he entered the lobby, he appeared flushed and frustrated and I quickly brought him back to my office. We both sat down and I leaned toward him, and I shifted into a clinical crisis debriefing mindset as I would when preparing to work with someone who has suffered a traumatic event.

"Tell me what happened," I said quietly.

"They made me a birthday cake," he said quietly.

"And then what happened," I said, waiting for the most terrible, horrible details of the event to come out.

"Then they sang happy birthday to me," he said quietly.

"And then what happened," I said, still waiting for the worst.

"That was it," he said in a matter-of-fact tone.

"And why was this so hard for you?" I asked, puzzled.

"Because today isn't my birthday," he said flatly. "My birthday is months away. I can't believe they did this," he said, shaking his head and staring down at the floor.

Neurotypical individuals would more than likely interpret this event as non-threatening and as a message of friendship and camaraderie. This type of joking is common among members of groups such as sports teams and is often part of building cohesiveness among the group members. The young man's father shared with me later that the baseball team did not mean any harm at all in this action, in fact, this act was done with kindness and wanting to connect with the young man on a deeper level. His father stated that the team members recognized that the young man was "different" and wanted to acknowledge that he was part of the group, and decided to celebrate his birthday on that day because his real birthday was not during the baseball season.

This incident demonstrates how the young man's inability to correctly interpret his teammates actions left him feeling as though they were attacking him even though they were actually trying to do the very opposite. He felt as though they were making fun of him by giving him a birthday cake and singing "Happy Birthday" because in his mind it was completely illogical to do something such as this when it was *not* the person's real birthday. This young man told me later that when his teammates did that, it felt like something was wrong with not only the action but with *him* and explained to me that "once they did that there was nothing I could do to stop them." The emotional aftereffect of this incident was that the young man was depressed for a few days, although he did return to the team and finish the season. No amount of persuasion by me or his parents could convince him that this was a "joke" and could not see the humor or friendliness in the incident. However, this experience was useful for him as I ended up seeing him a few years later and we discussed similar situations that he had encountered as his social world expanded following high school.

The second characteristic of adolescents diagnosed with AS that makes them vulnerable to the negative effects of bullying and social rejection is alexithymia. Alexithymia is the inability to recognize and give meaning to emotional signals in oneself and others (Fitzgerald and Bellgrove, 2006). I have found that for adolescents diagnosed with AS, alexithymia often leads them to either exhibit shutdown behaviors such as not speaking or social withdrawal, or exhibiting explosive behaviors such as lashing out in fits of rage. Individuals diagnosed with AS tend to be confused by emotions and can easily become overwhelmed by them. For adolescents diagnosed with AS, recognizing their own feelings as well as attempting to understand emotional signals leaves them feeling out of place and mentally disorganized. Thus, when a situation arises where the adolescent diagnosed with AS needs to communicate with others for help or comfort, there is an inability to do so (Fitzgerald and Bellgrove, 2006), such as in the case of bullying. In a world where the silence of children and adolescents is rewarded and reinforced by adults it is important for the therapist to be mindful of helping the adolescent diagnosed with AS to find their voice. It is just as important to educate parents/caregivers as well as school personnel that just because the adolescent does not react does not mean that they are not affected or that the bullying or teasing does not bother them.

For some adolescents diagnosed with AS, the complications of alexithymia create a torrent of confusing emotions that results in the adolescent becoming physically and verbally explosive and lashing out at those around them. I worked with one young man diagnosed with AS who experienced routine teasing by classmates. Like many individuals diagnosed with AS, he had dealt with it by shutting down verbally and physically, which ramped up the bullying and made him a frequent target. However, one day he lashed out and physically attacked one of the bullies, which of course brought a hailstorm of negative attention as well as a referral to me for help. Comments such as "He was such a nice boy" and "I never thought he would do such a terrible thing," were frequent in the follow up that I did with the school personnel, and it was difficult for me to not react as a result of these idiotic comments as I pondered how long these adults would have lasted in this young man's personal hell that he had existed in for so long. For adolescents diagnosed with AS who may resort to lashing out, it is important for the therapist to educate parents/caregivers and school personnel that this can actually be seen as a strength in that the adolescent is trying to do *something* with the energy that comes from the internalized and confusing emotions, as well as defending him/herself.

Theme Three: Social Skills Deficits

The social-skills deficit of the individual diagnosed with AS is well known and is a hallmark characteristic of AS. The difficulties that social-skills deficits bring for the adolescent diagnosed with AS are compounded by the rapid physical, mental, and emotional growth that naturally occurs during adolescence, as well as by the importance that social skills play during this phase of development (Barnhill, 2001). For parents/caregivers of the adolescent diagnosed with AS, these social-skills deficits bring added pressure and frustration as the behaviors (or lack thereof) can no longer be ignored or explained away as easily as when the adolescent was a child. As a child grows into an adolescent, society expects more of the adolescent and the social landscape becomes more vast and complicated. Most parents/caregivers of adolescents diagnosed with AS that I speak with are also very concerned with the teen's future development and often these parents/caregivers have fears related to the adolescent not developing into a successful adult because of severe social-skills deficits. Therapist working with parents/caregivers of adolescents diagnosed with AS should not minimize these fears when they are voiced by parents/caregivers. Research supports the validity of these fears in that the social-skills deficits of young people diagnosed with AS do not magically disappear, and in fact the deficits endure into adulthood where employment and social relationships are severely affected (Rao, Beidel, and Murray, 2008).

I discussed in Chapter Four how mindblindness, alexithymia, and problems with joint attention cause disruptions in the child diagnosed with AS to understand and interact with the social environment, and these elements continue to cause disruptions during the adolescent years. Add to this the extra pressure from parents/caregivers, teachers, and school personnel who expect more adult-like behavior from the adolescent, as well as the increase in overt bullying and social rejection from peers in both verbal and physical forms. One can see the seemingly insurmountable difficulties the adolescent faces. Munro (2010) and Attwood (1998) note how children diagnosed with AS "seem to invoke the maternal or predatory instinct in others" (p. 161). The therapist working with adolescents diagnosed with AS must be able to help the adolescent gain better social skills despite the barriers that are present. Parents/caregivers must be reminded to be patient with the process and also be willing to be part of the process. While the barriers seem insurmountable, it is my belief that the adolescent diagnosed with AS can learn better social skills with a skilled, empathic therapist and parents/caregivers who are committed to being part of the social skill learning process.

Theme Four: Emotional Regulation Difficulties and Emotional Immaturity

Social-skills deficits and social problems are at the forefront of discussions regarding the struggles of individuals diagnosed with AS; however, in recent years there has been a call in the literature for the need to understand and address the issue of the inability of individuals diagnosed with AS to regulate emotions (Gellar, 2005; Laurent and Rubin, 2004). Emotional regulation is an important part of successfully navigating the social world. Understanding our own emotions, recognizing and understanding the emotions of others, and being able to express emotions are key elements of living and connecting with others and successfully maintaining those connections. Gellar (2005) points out that our emotional nature comprises much more than feelings. Emotions are part of an intricate physiological network that encompasses memory, survival, and interactions with others. For the adolescent diagnosed with AS, the inability to regulate emotions is the cause many of the social-skills deficits observed by others in the outside world. Therapists who work with adolescents diagnosed with AS often encounter an initial referral due to social-skills deficits, but soon find that the real problem lies in the inability of the young person to successfully regulate emotion. I do believe, however that social-skills deficits and the inability to regulate emotion are separate therapeutic themes that require differentiated approaches, but a great deal of overlap exists between the two.

One of the main issues resulting in the inability of the adolescent diagnosed with AS to regulate emotion is the asynchrony and disruption in the physical, neurological, and sensory development that occurred when the adolescent was a child. For instance, some areas develop rapidly while others remain stagnant. A visual picture of this would be to imagine a child whose legs and head grew very rapidly but the feet and trunk did not, along with arms that grew to adult size in just a few short years but the hands remained childlike. This person would have great difficulty moving around and performing daily tasks and would appear clumsy and awkward. While the person would be able to adapt and survive, the person's ability to thrive would be greatly hampered. Another picture that I use with parents to represent the common advanced intellectual abilities yet stunted emotional and social development of the child or adolescent diagnosed with AS is to think of a tiny go-cart with a dragster engine attached to it. The go-cart will have great power due to the engine but the other parts will be ill-equipped to handle the tremendous strain that will result due to the over-powerful engine. The wheels are too small, the frame cannot handle the torque and force of the thrust of the engine, and the result will be a disaster due to the lack of balance. However, when a frame and other parts such as tires and steering mechanisms are specially designed to handle the power of the engine, the result is a beautiful balance of the appropriate parts working together. Thus, our children and adolescents diagnosed with AS develop out of balance, and when one considers the tremendous challenges this asynchronous and disrupted development brings, it is a wonder they function as well as they do!

Another disruption during development of the adolescent diagnosed with AS that contributes to asynchrony is the constant triggering of the sympathetic nervous system. I have previously discussed the issue of the triggering of the sympathetic nervous system (fight-or-flight) and the impact that a sustained, threatening influence has on the brain of the developing child diagnosed with AS. This can further complicate and cause even greater imbalance due to windows of growth and development being missed because of the brain being overloaded from being in fight-or-flight mode. An additional complication is that parts of the brain become fixed and less moldable during development due to the constant firing of the sympathetic nervous system. These parts of the brain, mainly those areas that deal with higher-order thinking as well as interpreting danger in the environment tend to be less plastic; that is, these areas of the brain become resistant to switching back to the parasympathetic state even when the threatening stimuli is not present (Baron-Cohen, 2006; Crenshaw & Mordock, 2005; Rothschild, 2000). Upper-level schooling places great strain on the parts of the brain that deal with "executive functioning" (long-term planning, organization, etc.) because projects and assignments require more long-term planning and abstract reasoning. Adolescents diagnosed with AS struggle with these tasks because they have a hard time breaking the task into smaller parts (Barnhill, 2004).

I share with my students that a competent therapist must multi-task when working with an adolescent diagnosed with AS because of this unbalanced development. It is important to know which areas have developed more rapidly than others, which areas are functioning well, and which areas are delayed. It is also important to ascertain the adolescent's and parent/caregiver's level of coping and resilience against stress, as well as the amount of bombardment on the adolescent from external forces such as bullying, teasing, or undue pressure from schools and family members. It is the job of the therapist to pull the child or adolescent diagnosed with AS up the developmental ladder and help bring these unbalanced and asynchronous areas into balance as much as possible. This is why I am passionate about the use of play with children and adolescents diagnosed with AS because it provides an amazing tool to help bring healing, growth, and connection in creating a beautiful balance where before only broken and mismatched pieces littered the developmental landscape.

Emotional immaturity is another commonly occurring phenomenon observable in adolescents diagnosed with AS and stems from the inability to regulate emotion. Emotional immaturity can be displayed through tantrums and outbursts that are out of proportion to the situation. For instance, one young lady about fourteen years old who was diagnosed with AS was referred to me by her parents because she would display violent tantrums if things did not go her way. She would become angry and tantrum if her mother would not buy her a specific brand of cereal, or she would begin crying which then turned into screaming if her socks were not on her feet just right prior to putting on her shoes. Her parents, like many parents/caregivers of children and adolescents diagnosed with AS, had stopped taking her places because of the fear of a tantrum in a public place.

Emotional immaturity is evidenced in many other ways in adolescents diagnosed with AS. Separation-anxiety, the fear of being separated from a specific person or persons is very common in adolescents diagnosed with AS. Many young people that I have worked with who are diagnosed with AS experience a bout of separation-anxiety around the time of entering middle school and sometimes when the adolescent transitions from middle school to high school. This can be the result of bullying or teasing, or because of the transition to a new place with a new routine and a lot more people. Middle school also represents a change in structure. Instead of one or two teachers, there are sometimes as many as seven or eight. In addition, there are more social demands with increasingly complex social dynamics that have the potential to overwhelm the adolescent diagnosed with AS.

Emotional immaturity is often observable in the social interactions of adolescents diagnosed with AS. Adolescents as well as children diagnosed with AS tend to desire relationships with those much younger than their own peer group. An adolescent boy with a fourteen-year-old body would rather play with Lego sets with the six-year-old boy next door, or a sixteen-year-old girl would rather pretend she is a princess and play with Barbie dolls with her four-year-old cousin instead of going to the mall with classmates. These instances reflect what is going on emotionally inside the adolescent diagnosed with AS and shed light on their level of comfortableness in social situations. I often encounter parents/caregivers who are very concerned about this and share their failed attempts in forcing their adolescent diagnosed with AS to socialize with young people their own age. These attempts usually end in frustration both for the adolescent diagnosed with AS and the parent/caregiver. I work to help them understand that this is normal considering the interplay of alexithymia, mindblindness, and joint-attention deficits. I encourage the parent/caregiver to continue exposing the adolescent diagnosed with AS to social situations with their peer group; however, I also encourage them to adopt a "so what?" attitude when their adolescent does end up socializing with younger children.

A "so what" attitude may sound harsh, but sharing this with parents comes from conversations with young people who have told me that when they interact with younger children they feel like they are with people who understand them. I have also spoken with adolescents diagnosed with AS who have told me that they like how younger kids "listen" when they are showing them how to do something, and that they like to "teach" younger children what they know. I noted an increase in self-worth in the adolescents diagnosed with AS when they talked about these interactions and I have used these interactions as a way to work on joint-attention deficits, mindblindness, and alexithymia. I teach parents that social interaction, regardless of whether or not it is with the adolescent's peer group or with younger children, is a positive influence in the adolescent's development. This is another example of how society places pressure on parents for their children to be "normal" (even though no one knows what this really means) and this pressure is a significant source of guilt and shame for parents and adds to their fears when their child does not fit in the "box." I will discuss this phenomenon later in the section on family stress of families who have adolescents diagnosed with AS.

Theme Five: Transitions of the Adolescent Diagnosed with Asperger's Syndrome: Middle School, High School, and Adulthood

The adolescent diagnosed with AS faces many obstacles on the path to adulthood in the form of social challenges, relationship challenges, as well as increased academic demands. Transition points represent challenges for individuals diagnosed with AS in moving from elementary to middle school, middle school to high school, and finally from high school to adulthood. These transitions are accompanied by developmental changes such as physical, mental, and emotional transformations that are often asynchronous in nature and make the time of adolescence even more chaotic for the adolescent diagnosed with AS. Parents/caregivers have a front row seat in observing the difficulties of the adolescent diagnosed with AS due to increased academic demands, more social and relational challenges, and the difficulties that stem from emotional immaturity and alexithymia.

The neurotypical adolescent's physical, mental, and emotional development tends to be fairly synchronous and even. While some unevenness of development is present in all adolescents (for instance, emotional immaturity in boys), most of the key developmental areas have evened out or "caught up" by the end of adolescence as the adolescent approaches adulthood. The neurotypical adolescent usually becomes more independent as adolescence ends, and as a result of better social skills and increased social awareness the neurotypical adolescent often possesses a readiness to take on new transitional challenges such as entering college or the work force. The neurotypical individual enters adulthood with a skillset that provides a foundation for learning as development and experience mesh together and leads the young person toward opportunities for success.

For the adolescent diagnosed with AS, the reality of approaching adulthood and the thought of independence are often accompanied by feelings of dread, confusion, and apathy. Because of the asynchronous nature of development that causes disruptions in cognitive, emotional, and social development, the adolescent diagnosed with AS often struggles with life's transitions. For the adolescent diagnosed with AS, the world is already a place that is unpredictable and ever changing, complete with new demands and situations that are threatening and unbearable at times. One young man diagnosed with AS who was about to transition from middle school to high school told me that he was "terrified" because his middle school experience was very painful due to severe bullying. Another young man told me he felt "paralyzed" by fear due to his parents' wish for him to get a job during the summer before his senior year in high school. Yet another young man who was home-schooled and nearing his twentieth birthday became angry with me and walked out of the office when we met with his parents to help formulate ideas to help him toward independence. The root of his behavior was fear in thinking of his daily routine being changed, and the thought of responsibility, such as a job or college classes, created feelings of sheer terror.

I do not want to paint a gloomy picture of adulthood for the adolescent diagnosed with AS who is quickly approaching adulthood. Tantam (1991) states that once the difficult socialization periods of adolescence are over, adults diagnosed with AS appear to continue to improve in their socializations "well into their twenties and thirties" (p. 179). There are many people diagnosed with AS who go on to successful careers, establish social relationships, and even marry. These individuals diagnosed with AS tend to have great resilience and find ways to turn the challenges of AS into strengths. However, research does suggest that many individuals diagnosed with AS have difficulties in the transition to adulthood in the areas of relationships, achieving independence, and maintaining employment (Tantum, 1991; Rao et al., 2008). A common theme that seems to be a constant is that of support during the major life transitions. Those individuals diagnosed with AS who do well tend to have either family or some other relationship in their life that buoys them when the waves get rough. One young man that I discuss later in Chapter Seven weathered many storms during middle school and high school and entered college with the passion of being a special education teacher. He required support and modifications to help him through his transition to adulthood and continues to need various levels of those supports. However, while at times the progress is slow, he is learning and I am happy to say he is progressing well. Welkowitz and Baker (2005) share encouraging stories of success of young adults who are in college but also point out that these young adults diagnosed with AS require supports to successfully navigate the college environment and achieve the goal of getting a college degree.

Theme Six: Family Stress and Challenges

I discussed in Chapter Four some of the challenges that families encounter with children diagnosed with AS. I believe it is important to address various forms of stress and challenges that families encounter who have an adolescent diagnosed with AS because families play a large role in helping the adolescent face the transitions of the adolescent years. I mentioned how many parents can carry a great deal of guilt and shame (Lozzi-Toscano, 2004) because of the nature of AS, and I find that many parents allow the pressure of society's expectations to discourage them and miss the miracles that come with having an adolescent diagnosed with AS. Parents must cognitively shift out of a "scarcity mindset" (looking at life through the lens of what is lacking) and adopt an "abundance mindset" (being grateful for what is present and see potential for future growth). However, many parents are still experiencing a great deal of grief and denial regarding the reality of their child or adolescent living with AS.

I encounter parents who secretly believe the myth that when their child reaches adolescence, the social, educational, and emotional challenges of the child diagnosed with AS will magically disappear. Other parents/ caregivers yearn and hope for a "cure" and try the latest treatments found among those in the autism community. I adopt a learning attitude with these parents and encourage them to try various diets, natural/herbal treatments, or behavioral approaches but caution them to seek out documented research that supports the treatment that they want to try. As they read, I read; as they learn, I learn; and as they attempt to try something new, I observe with them and hope with them. I admire these parents and caregivers. I pray for them. I love them. For any parent/caregiver of a child or adolescent with special needs, regardless of what those needs may be, life is hard. For the parent/ caregiver of the adolescent diagnosed with AS, there are not only the physical, mental, and emotional difficulties that create the social challenges, but there are the fears of the future and the dreaded unknown that every parent experiences in wondering what will happen to their adolescent diagnosed with AS.

One single mother of an adolescent talked with me one day about her fears of the future for her son, a sixteen-year-old who was diagnosed with AS at the age of five. With tears in her eyes she told me:

I can't even begin to picture him being on his own, holding down a job . . . I gave up on thinking of him going to college years ago. I do everything for him now, and it is as if he doesn't even care or even knows what he will do. He is sixteen and it is as if he is a child. I worry daily that if I die he will be homeless and be killed on the streets. What am I going to do?

This particular mother was a single mother who had adopted her son from a family member when he was a baby and she was approaching retirement age. She lived on a fixed income with no ability to pay for her son to be able to have his own apartment or to be able to pay for special treatment. Her lament for her son contained not only fear regarding the future but also sadness regarding the inability of her son to function independently.

My passion in helping adolescents diagnosed with AS to better understand themselves and others and find their place in the world spills over to wanting to help ease the burdens of parents and caregivers. I shared in Chapter Four of the extra stress and strain on the relationships of the parents/caregivers of these young people (Hartley et al., 2010). I want to calm their fears as well as lead them to greater connection with their adolescent. Many parents/caregivers simply have a desire to connect with someone who will listen and understand their feelings. One mother told me that she had stopped talking with friends with neurotypical children because one of them remarked, "It sounds like you really hate your kid." The truth was that she loved her son very much but needed to vent her frustration with his stubbornness, clumsiness, and lack of academic progress. I connected her with a local support group to help give her a connection with people who would understand and not judge her emotions.

Anyone who spends time with parents of teens, whether neurotypical or diagnosed with AS, will hear the parent(s) venting about the various struggles and challenges of raising an adolescent. As someone who lives with a neurotypical adolescent I have commiserated with other parents about my being awestruck that this young man, who is so resourceful and brilliant, could walk past a trash can at least twenty times in one day and not think to pull it (on wheels, even!) from the street to the house. I often hear parents of adolescents begin a session with, "O.K. just let me vent about this kid for a few minutes!" Most parents, myself included, vent frustration out of love for the adolescent. In fact, in the same breath one will usually hear about some great achievement or ability of the adolescent immediately following the frustration, "Really . . . he really is a great kid . . ."

Yet I hear from parents of adolescents diagnosed with AS that when they begin talking about their frustration and struggles to neighbors or friends with neurotypical children they are met with apathy, judgmental responses, or shunning. Thus many parents of adolescents diagnosed with AS begin to avoid social interactions much like their adolescent and isolate themselves away from friends with neurotypical children and even away from family gatherings. These feelings of rejection begin to grow, and deep resentment can begin to set in, eating away like a silent cancer inside the individual parent or caregiver; inside the foundation of the marriage or intimate partnerships; and even within the family system itself. While venting of frustration is very positive and healthy, therapists must pay attention to the themes found therein to assess for the level of coping skills and negative aspects that often accompany parenting an adolescent diagnosed with AS such as despair or excessive fatigue.

When I find myself with a parent/caregiver of an adolescent diagnosed with AS who is venting I pay careful attention to the language that is used, to the emotions that are being elicited (this includes body language and physical manifestations of the emotions, like tears, etc.) how long the venting lasts, and how the venting ends. Does the parent/caregiver appear renewed or refreshed after venting, or is there a heavy weight of grief and despair that is left over following the release of frustration. If the latter, the parent/caregiver needs a dose of encouragement. I am a firm believer that therapists play a very important role in encouraging the parents/caregivers of the adolescents diagnosed with AS that come for therapy. The parent/caregivers are on the front line of attempting to meet the needs of the adolescent diagnosed with AS and many of them constantly question their abilities and wonder if they are doing "the right thing." We must encourage, we must empathize, we must let them know that we are with the parent/caregiver to hear their frustrations, offer them hope, and provide answers to their many questions (Munro, 2010).

A final piece worth mentioning when working with the families of adolescents diagnosed with AS is dealing with the frustrations of neurotypical sibling(s) that are often part of the landscape in these families. I discussed in earlier chapters how the sibling(s) of children diagnosed with AS must learn to cope with their unique sibling, and for the sibling(s) of adolescents diagnosed with AS it is no different. The sibling(s) must deal with the challenges that AS brings, and every member of the family is affected in different ways. I have found that parents tend to deal with frustrations of the sibling(s) in two ways. One way is viewing any voicing of frustration by the sibling(s) as mean or cruel and not allowing any one in the family to complain. Thus, the sibling(s) begin to build resentment and feel as though they have no voice. The other extreme of parents dealing with the frustrations of the sibling(s) of the adolescent diagnosed with AS is to allow the adolescent diagnosed with AS to become a scapegoat for all the family's problems. In this scenario, the parent's frustrations are channeled through the neurotypical sibling(s) indirectly at the adolescent diagnosed with AS. The adolescent diagnosed with AS is left to fend for himself/herself and often learns a reactive, defensive stance. Without the ability to modulate emotion, the adolescent diagnosed with AS appears to be aggressive, when in actuality the family dynamics have caused the adolescent to perceive himself/herself to be isolated and alone.

The sibling(s) of the adolescent diagnosed with AS need to be able to voice frustration and to be given coping skills. A therapist working with the adolescent diagnosed with AS can easily forget that the sibling(s) must deal with the challenges of having a brother or sister diagnosed with AS. I have spent time with many siblings of adolescents diagnosed with AS and often hear their frustration related to the emotional outbursts, unpredictable behavior, and odd and peculiar ways that their sibling diagnosed with AS sees the world. Some voice feelings of embarrassment over the behavior or immaturity of their unique sibling, others feel pressure to take care of and protect the adolescent diagnosed with AS. Parents can add to this pressure by telling the sibling(s) that they are in charge of their unique sibling diagnosed with AS, or by focusing on the abilities/talents of the sibling(s) and ignoring the adolescent diagnosed with AS. This can be compounded by that fact that the adolescent diagnosed with AS often lacks the ability to adequately voice their wants and desires and hopes that the parent/caregiver will read their mind.

One family I worked with had an adolescent diagnosed with AS and two younger neurotypical siblings. The younger siblings were very active in extracurricular activities and each weekend the family spent great amounts of time at the younger siblings' events. The adolescent diagnosed with AS shared with me when we were examining his interests that he had a great desire to be involved in chess competitions that took place on the weekend but was told that the younger siblings' events were more important because "they were very good" at the extracurricular activities. When I explored this with the parents, they admitted that they had become so accustomed to focusing on the deficits in their adolescent diagnosed with AS for so long that they did not even realize how much they were favoring their neurotypical children's interests and ignoring those of the adolescent diagnosed with AS. We worked on finding a balance so that all of the children could be involved in extracurricular activities but that the adolescent diagnosed with AS could pursue his interest in being involved in chess competitions. This was very instrumental in the adolescent diagnosed with AS experiencing new levels of self-worth as well as creating opportunities for relationship building between the adolescent and the parents.

The therapist plays an important role in helping the family of the adolescent diagnosed with AS voice frustrations; helps the family better understand the differences, gifts, talents, and needs of the adolescent diagnosed with AS;

helps the family build deeper connection and relationship among family members; and helps the family learn important coping skills. I am passionate about the health and coping skills of the families of the adolescents diagnosed with AS because I believe that the family is a key foundation for the teen's emotional and social development as the adolescent faces the many transitions of adolescence that lead toward adulthood. I will discuss specific ways that the therapist working with adolescents diagnosed with AS can help build family connection and strengthen the family foundation through play in the next chapter.

Chapter 7

Play Therapy with Adolescents Diagnosed with Asperger's Syndrome

THE RATIONALE FOR PLAY THERAPY WITH ADOLESCENTS

Play therapy is usually thought of as a treatment approach for children only, but there is a good amount of research that suggests it is also useful for adolescents (Gallo-Lopez & Schaefer, 2005). Play therapy is a way to engage adolescents who sometimes find traditional therapy approaches boring and threatening. Play therapy is especially useful for adolescents that are regressed or have missed out on parts of childhood due to trauma or abuse. For adolescents struggling with attachment issues, play can be a chance to explore deeper parts of thinking and emotion in relationship with the therapist in a fun and inviting way. Directive play can be effective in breaking down defensive attitudes that adolescents sometimes have and foster a sense of connection and trust between themselves and a therapist. Even an activity as simple as throwing a ball back and forth has powerful implications in building trust (Norton and Norton, 1997). Throwing a ball with another is a test of trust in that the one throwing the ball could try to inflict harm and vice versa. I often encounter adolescents that "test" me by throwing a ball very hard at me and are sometimes surprised not only at my ability to calmly catch the ball but to also deliver it back with a smooth, nonthreatening rhythm. After a few sequences of throws, the angry defensiveness has usually lessened and the foundation of trust becomes strengthened.

Adolescents diagnosed with AS have several characteristics that make them prime candidates for play therapy. One characteristic is emotional immaturity that is often present in those diagnosed with AS and results in the adolescent being interested in toys and games that are geared for children of younger ages. For instance, a fifteen-year-old male diagnosed with AS loved to play Pokémon, the video game and card game. During the second session, he brought a carton full of Pokémon cards and showed me his prized cards which were very valuable to him. He talked incessantly about this imaginary world and the various powers of each character, and shared in details about each of the video games and how each one was unique. His sixteenth birthday was weeks away and his distraught parents were in a quandary about what to do about their son's Pokémon obsession. I had seen an eight-year-old neurotypical boy a few weeks earlier who showed the same passion as the fifteen-year-old boy diagnosed with AS and it struck me how similar the levels of interest and passion were between the two. The adolescent's interest in Pokémon made play therapy a natural approach in building rapport and trust as well as creating metaphors for emotional and social growth.

Another characteristic of adolescents diagnosed with AS that makes play therapy an effective treatment approach is the difficulty many individuals diagnosed with AS have verbalizing thoughts and feelings. Play becomes the vehicle of communication and can help lessen the frustration of the adolescent who struggles with putting thoughts and feelings into words by allowing the action of play to speak for him or her. Play serves to lessen the threatening nature of therapy as many adolescents in general can often see it as a frustrating and terrorizing experience because, in their own words, "they never know what to say." Play can also relieve pressure from the therapist who can feel very intimidated by an adolescent who refuses to speak or interact on any level. For adolescents diagnosed with AS, social interactions and settings with people with whom they are not familiar with create tension and can trigger an impulse to withdraw and shutdown in order to feel safe. Play is a non-threatening activity that allows the adolescent diagnosed with AS to communicate in their own style and at their own pace, while trust and rapport are built between them and the therapist in a gradual, steady manner.

A final reason that makes play a viable option for treating adolescents diagnosed with AS in therapy is the importance of familiarity and predictability that produces a sense of safety for these unique and amazing individuals. A sense of safety is very important for individuals diagnosed with AS, because many see new situations and new people as threatening. Many adolescents diagnosed with AS who have experienced bullying do not trust adults other than their parents because these adults have not kept them safe in situations where they were physically and emotionally harmed. Play is powerful because it is familiar, especially if it involves a stereotyped interest of the adolescent. Play can also be predictable because the adolescent is the one who is in control of the activity and the course of the play is determined by the adolescent diagnosed with AS. I have several adolescents diagnosed with AS who come to my office who expect the same toys and activities to be used each time, and many have told me they feel "safe" at my office because the toys are "always" there and they know what they are going to be able to do.

THE ROLE OF THE THERAPIST AND IN PLAY THERAPY WITH ADOLESCENTS DIAGNOSED WITH ASPERGER'S SYNDROME

Therapists who use play therapy with adolescents in general, whether the adolescent is diagnosed with AS or not, should be prepared to adopt an active, directive approach to get the play process going. The cultural climate, coupled with the advances of technology is forcing children to grow up faster than ever and many adolescents have received the message from parents, teachers, and the culture in general that they are not supposed to play and many are ashamed that they desire to do so. I have encountered many girls between the ages of ten and thirteen who tell me that they still want to play with Barbie dolls but feel embarrassed to do so and worry that their parents or friends would find out and "think I am weird." I have met sixteen-year-old boys who still want to play with GI Joe figures and act out battles in the sand box but who are terrified at the thought of parents or peers finding out. As a grown man who engages in the wonder and magic of play every day, this saddens me very much. No wonder our world is in the state it is in, and no wonder children, teens, and adults are crushed under the weight of stress. Schools continue to remove free play opportunities from the curriculum in elementary school, and adolescents have few outlets to release their inner need to play because of the pressure of the culture to grow up and the fear of being teased by peers. Ironically, a phenomenon that I have witnessed in my work with young couples is the male in his mid-twenties to early thirties who is obsessed with online computer and video games, to the point of losing his job and neglecting his husband and fatherly duties.

Play therapy with children and adolescents diagnosed with AS tends to be more directive in nature due to the deficits in spontaneous and imaginative play that are common in children diagnosed with AS (Lu, et al., 2009). The directive therapist acts as a guide and model in inviting the adolescent diagnosed with AS to play. Milgrom (2005) discusses the importance of this invitation of the therapist to the adolescent to enter the realm of play, and states that the therapist should model a spirit of playfulness, demonstrate enthusiasm for play, and have a sense of humor as the session begins to unfold. The therapist should prepare themselves for the reaction of the adolescent, which may range from joy and laughter, to annoyance and coolness. The therapist must not react negatively nor respond with judgment and remember that engaging in the play ultimately remains "the adolescent's choice" (Milgrom,

2005, p. 7). I must admit that in my eagerness to invite adolescents diagnosed with AS into the play process there have been times where I was too forceful in the invitation and perceived that it was "too much" for that particular adolescent based on their facial reactions and body language. I have adopted a much more laid-back approach, remembering that for individuals diagnosed with AS the emotions and behaviors of others, particularly those that they do not know, are often confusing as well as threatening.

Respect

I cannot say enough of the importance of the therapist showing respect for the adolescent diagnosed with AS who comes to therapy. While we as therapists have a vast array of research and knowledge available to us, each child, adolescent, and adult diagnosed with AS that we encounter is a unique human being and we must never forget this fact! When I began social-skills groups for adolescents diagnosed with AS I had a very humbling teaching moment. I had immersed myself in reading research regarding mindblindness and alexithymia and I was determined to make addressing these deficits a priority in this particular group. I had selected a few movie clips and some documentary footage that I had put together to show to the group to begin working on these common deficits. I would intermittently stop the movie clips to expand on what was going on to *make sure* that the group members understood. One of them finally stood up after I stopped the movie and shouted, "Just play the damn thing, we are not stupid, you know!" I realized that I had been immersed in so much research that I had forgotten to see my group member's individual characteristics and unique gifts and talents. I had made a fundamental error in that I was seeing them as one entity: Asperger's Syndrome, instead of unique people with intelligence, gifts, talents, interests, and emotions who just happened to be diagnosed with AS.

I have stumbled upon various websites that are set up by individuals diagnosed with AS and I read with interest the postings of these "Aspies" who write about their lives and their unique perspective of the world, as well as their struggles and triumphs. One set of postings that I read recently was on the topic of counseling and psychotherapy that many of these individuals were exposed to in their youth. This piqued my interest as a therapist because I am always intrigued by hearing people's experiences in therapy, and to know if the experience was helpful and if so, what made it helpful. If the person's experience was not a good one, I want to know that as well. One theme that was very interesting to me in the responses was that many of the young people diagnosed with AS felt that the therapist was condescending and that the sessions were so structured and rigid that the person felt stifled.

However, many wrote that when therapy was helpful there was an open and free style to the therapy process. Some wrote about being so smart that they were able to manipulate the therapist and that made the boring experience of therapy somewhat tolerable. I am saddened when I hear of a young person who was exposed to therapy and emerged feeling disrespected and devalued by a therapist. I understand that it is not the job of the therapist to make the adolescent like the therapist or like the process of therapy; in fact, I believe that at times the process may be hated by the adolescent and that is because the therapist is doing necessary work. However, I do believe that regardless of the adolescent's demeanor or opinion of the therapist or the process of therapy, the adolescent must be shown respect at all times. I think we as therapists should be paying attention to what people are saying in these posts on various websites because it can help ground us to that one basic premise that respect for our clients is a fundamental and necessary component for therapeutic growth.

PLAY THERAPY TO HELP BUILD SELF-WORTH IN THE ADOLESCENT DIAGNOSED WITH ASPERGER'S SYNDROME

Computer and Video Games

I discussed in Chapter Five how computer and video games can be very effective in working with children diagnosed with AS. The same is true for adolescents diagnosed with AS. I have found that adolescents diagnosed with AS are even more connected to computer and video games than are children, and with a heightened level of focus and intensity. Adolescents usually have more access to higher-level games because children are restricted from them. Parents of adolescents who love computer and video games usually have long since given up trying to restrict the adolescent diagnosed with AS from the mature rated games. Many of the parents rationalize their decision by citing that the computer and video games are often the teen's only real interest, and many are simply tired of fighting about it. Online gaming is very popular with adolescents diagnosed with AS, and adolescents usually spend much more time than children involved in online role-playing games (RPGs) such as RuneScape (Jagex, 2002) or World of Warcraft. These multiplayer RPGs have elaborate action sequences and intricate connections among players that tend to appeal to the adolescent diagnosed with AS. LeGoff (2004) and Attwood (1998) cite the importance of using stereotyped interests in the therapy process, and when I encounter an adolescent diagnosed with AS who is interested in a particular computer or video game I learn as much as I can about the game and invite the adolescent to bring in their game system or show me the game on the computer in the office.

It is important to note that the therapist does not have to be especially skilled in the game for the game to be used in the therapy session. There are simply too many games to keep track of and too many game systems for a single person to be adept at playing all of them. Allowing the adolescent to teach the therapist is a wonderful way to place the adolescent in the role of the expert and the therapist in the role of the pupil and also gets the therapist in the adolescent's world. It is a wonderful opportunity to build trust with the adolescent and to model patience and joint attention. I have experienced adolescents diagnosed with AS "lighting up" at the prospect of sharing their game with an adult who shows genuine interest in what the adolescent loves. I have witnessed an adolescent diagnosed with AS become more animated and talkative when sharing their game with me and it has led to a whole new world of metaphors that can be used to help the adolescent with emotional and social growth, as well as insight and judgment.

It is important to share with the parent or caregiver the purpose of using the games in the therapy sessions. Sometimes parents are very concerned about the obsessive nature of their adolescent's game playing and frown upon "spending good money" to have them bring their obsession into the therapy room where they hope that the therapist can "talk some sense into them and get them to stop playing the games." I use these comments and attitudes as a way to educate the parents about the nature of AS and why adolescents diagnosed with AS tend to be drawn to computer and video games. Discussing parenting styles and addressing the fears of parents and caregivers regarding computer and video games are beyond the scope of this book, but I do want to say that I believe in parents and caregivers setting limits and teaching self-discipline when it comes to computer and video games. However, for the individual diagnosed with AS the draw of the computer and video game system is intense and instantly rewarding. It is important for parents and caregivers to understand this, and rather than trying to completely squash the adolescent's interest (which I think is impossible), the parent or caregiver can learn to help the adolescent learn to self-limit and teach coping skills. Several adolescents diagnosed with AS have told me that it is through playing online computer games and talking with and connecting to others that they have begun to understand what friendship really means, as well as understanding the dynamics of loyalty, sacrifice, and empathy.

The process of using computer and video games with adolescents is similar to what I described in working with children diagnosed with AS. Perhaps the greatest value that computer and video games bring to therapy is the parallels between the games and life. The themes of challenges, going to the next level, completing a mission, relying on others, believing in oneself, and practice are all constants found in life and found in computer and video games. I recommend playing games with a two-player feature that helps build connection between the therapist and the adolescent diagnosed with AS. This connection provides a model for social-skills work to be done later by presenting opportunities for the ingredients of a social relationship (communication, forming a bond over a common interest, compromise, etc.) that can be examined and discussed. Playing a game together lays the groundwork for self-worth work, particularly when the adolescent is teaching the game to the therapist. Most adolescents I encounter enjoy demonstrating their skills and abilities when playing a game with which they are familiar, and this provides an excellent opportunity for self-worth building as therapy progresses. Single-player video games can be used as well. Single player games give the adolescent the opportunity to introduce the therapist to the game, and the therapist and adolescent can take turns if the adolescent wishes to do so.

I discussed in Chapter Five how metaphors from the game-playing experience can be applied in helping to build the self-worth of the individual diagnosed with AS. The metaphors that computer and video games provide for building self-worth are numerous (Hull, 2009). One powerful metaphor is the positive sense of accomplishment and uniqueness that having a specialized skill brings. Many adolescents diagnosed with AS have shared with me that they feel like "losers" compared to peers that excel at sports, play an instrument or dance, and are adept at handling social situations. Oftentimes these feelings have been present since childhood and become deeply entrenched in the adolescent years. Society rewards the fast runner who can hit or kick something far; or the singer or musician who shines on a stage. For many young people diagnosed with AS there is a sense of "being on my own planet" with very few stages on which they can shine based on the interests that the young person is drawn to. When a young person diagnosed with AS encounters the world of computer and video games, it is usually a "where has this been all my life?" phenomenon. The world of computer and video games is safe and ordered. It is a world to be discovered, a place where rewards abound for someone who is diligent and focused on exploring the vast hidden passages and levels that lie within this amazing creation.

I often explain to parents who are concerned that "this game is my teen's whole life" that it is probably impossible to replace such a powerful stimulus as a computer or video game with which the adolescent has formed a bond and that the adolescent is insistent upon playing. I work with the parents on limiting the game play and teaching balance, but I share with them that for many adolescents diagnosed with AS the computer or video game is like a lifeline that is not only a link to the outside world but a link to the adolescent's soul. I have had adolescents diagnosed with AS express to me that the computer or video game that they like is the only good thing that they can identify in their life and their ability to play the game is the only part of themselves that they see as "good." I use the positive feelings that the adolescent expresses that comes from being skilled at a computer or video game as well as the positive thoughts of believing that they are valuable and worthy in their gameplay. My goal is to take these positive thoughts and feelings that come from the game play and create a foundation of self-worth that can be a stabilizing force for the adolescent and create an inner confidence as the adolescent moves into new areas of transition and opportunities for mental, emotional, and social growth.

I worked with a nineteen-year-old young man who was diagnosed with AS when he was a child. Like many young people diagnosed with AS, he was experiencing a great deal of fear and difficulty transitioning into adulthood, which lead him to feeling very depressed because of attributing his inability to grow up to him "not being good enough." He was referred to counseling because of these emotional difficulties as well as demonstrating extreme resistance regarding his parents' wishes for him to secure a part-time job. He revealed to me early in therapy that his favorite game to play was Call of Duty Modern Warfare 2 (Activision, 2005) which is a first-person shooter game which resembles military combat, and he begged me to allow him to bring it in to the office. I agreed and we began to play the game during each session. He initially insisted on us playing against each other, and effortlessly destroyed me each time, which delighted him very much. He then wanted to play as a team, with he and I working together to secure our base from the enemies. While we played we discussed his fears about the future. He revealed themes of past abuse from bullies which made him afraid of meeting new people, as well as overwhelming feelings that he would "fail" because he felt like a "loser" for most of his life. Despite this, he was able to identify situations in his life where he had not "failed" and that not "everyone" was mean to him over the course of his life. I pulled various metaphors from the game such as using navigation points on the map to know which way to go, listening to the team leader to tell the players where the danger is, and using different weapons and accessories to get out of danger. I then asked him if he was an expert at the game the first time he played, or if he had improved in his playing. He told me that the first few times he played the game he "sucked" and could not even fire his weapon correctly. But after playing for some time he admitted that he had become very skilled and felt as though he could "go up against anybody and do well." "Are you ever afraid you are going to fail in the game?" I asked him. "Never," he quickly replied, "not now." I then used the metaphors of the game such as being prepared as a way to get him thinking about the next phase of life. I shared with him that no one enters the adult phase of life fully prepared; in fact, life is a perfect example of learning as one goes along and sometimes one temporarily "fails" but there is the opportunity to learn from failure just like in the game and one emerges from the process much smarter than when they began. We examined the "worst case scenarios" that he could think of that might happen if he had a job, and we looked at the "worst case scenarios" in the game and what one could do in those situations to do well. I was able to use this to build coping skills as we explored the options if he found himself in a "worst case scenario" at a job. I was stunned by how many metaphors came from this game as the young man and I continued to play. Eventually, he found the inner strength to conquer his fear and went on an interview and got a part-time job and made a friend the first day on the job. I met with him after he had the job for about a month and he admitted that while he was scared initially, he was able to look back and see that there was really nothing to be afraid of. I am hopeful that from going through this experience this young man will be able to face other challenges that life's transitions will bring.

I worked with one young man diagnosed with AS who was fifteen years old and an avid player of the game RuneScape (Jagex, 2002), an online multiplayer RPG in which one amasses abilities and possessions in a medieval world. As one plays the game, there are various activities one must perform to acquire skills and the more skills one has, the more land, possessions, and power one gains. Through testing, it was revealed that this young man's IQ was very high, but he also had battled depression for much of his childhood and it had carried over to adolescence. The emotional and social turbulence of adolescence would at times cause his depression to get worse, and he shared many of his social difficulties with me early in the therapy sessions. This young man had a very low self-worth and examination of his thinking process revealed an external locus of control in that he attributed his negative social experiences to his lack of ability and saw himself as the reason for his difficulties which resulted in depressive thinking patterns, much like Barnhill (2001) and Barnhill and Myles (2001) described. Instead of seeing himself as being capable of acquiring skills to become better socially adept and that he had the power to change his thinking, this young man simply saw himself as "terrible" and as a "really bad person," and at one point wondered if he "deserved" to be treated "like an outcast."

Barnhill (2001) suggested that "attribution re-training" (p. 51) may be helpful in helping adolescents diagnosed with AS such as this young man shift from an external locus of control resulting in learned helplessness to an internal locus of control and that would empower the adolescent as well as avoid negative self-attributions that result in depressive thinking. When I discovered that RuneScape (Jagex, 2002) was an integral part of this young man's life, I immersed myself in the game and learned as much as I could. I found that it was a proverbial "gold mine" for positive metaphors that would help in attribution re-training. The young man had been playing RuneScape (Jagex, 2002) for some time and had amassed a great amount of possessions and status within the game. He shared with me that he had risen to a very high rank in the game and that in the game he was very highly admired and esteemed. He shared that he felt good about himself when playing the game because of the respect and status that it brought, and was proud of the dedicated, sometimes tedious work he had performed to achieve his rank. I used these positive affirmations as a foundation to build upon and to help him understand that it was not the game that brought those positive thoughts and feelings, but it was *him* thinking positive that led to his positive feelings. I also constructed parallels between the game of RuneScape (Jagex, 2002) and life, focusing on themes of hard work, challenges, learning, relying on others, utilizing problem-solving skills, and patience. I made the connection that learning to do well in the social world for him would be much like playing a challenging computer or video game: There would be learning, challenges, figuring out situations, dealing with disappointment and fear, and not giving up. Finally, I was able to help the young man see that it was not him that was the reason for his social difficulties; it was simply that he had not been playing the social "game" with as many tools as he could because those were not yet developed. I helped him understand that the person whom he really liked and was proud of in the game of RuneScape (Jagex, 2002) was the same person who could apply the positive thinking that he exhibited during his gameplay to himself in life situations. Slowly, his negative attributions began to shift. The parallels drawn between the game and life were helpful for him to have as a reference point for remembering that he was valuable and had a great deal of worth, not just as a RuneScape (Jagex, 2002) player but as a person.

Art

I discussed the value of art in Chapter Five and I want to include it here as I have found it to be an important way to build self-worth in adolescents diagnosed with AS. Having an adolescent draw or make a figure of themselves through the mediums of drawing, painting, and sculpting allow the adolescent to "look" at themselves in new and positive ways. The therapist can also find out how the adolescent sees others and views relationships by having the adolescent draw, paint, or sculpt individuals in their family or peer group. One young lady was referred to me due to depression, and after meeting with her

I discovered that her self-worth was very low. She saw herself as less then valuable because of the social rejection that she had experienced during the course of her childhood and early adolescent years. However, she was interested in art and enjoyed drawing and I used her love of drawing to get her to create pictures that represented the parts of herself that she liked and the parts of herself that she did not like. I also had her draw pictures that represented various emotions such as fear and sadness when others had rejected her. She was able to find value and worth in herself when she drew and created through art, and this provided valuable material to help her generalize those positive attributions to herself in other situations, not just when she was creating through art. Through her art we were also able to examine how she saw others as threatening and better than she, and this provided material to help her change those perceptions. Over time this young lady was able improve her self-worth and as a result her depression decreased and her parents and teachers noted improvement in her mood.

PLAY THERAPY TO HELP THE ADOLESCENT DIAGNOSED WITH ASPERGER'S SYNDROME DEAL WITH BULLYING AND SOCIAL REJECTION

I have written extensively about the mental and emotional devastation that bullying and social rejection brings upon individuals diagnosed with AS. For adolescents diagnosed with AS, the bullying and social rejection they encounter simply cements the self-loathing, fear, and confusion that was born in childhood and locks it into place leaving the adolescent physically, mentally, emotionally, and socially paralyzed. The therapist must be able to help break apart this terrible residue and help the adolescent grow and learn to live without fear so that they can learn better social skills. I have discussed how fear triggers the sympathetic nervous system ("fight or flight") and disrupts the ability to learn and grow, instead leaving the individual in survival mode. The following techniques are designed to help the adolescent diagnosed with AS deal with fear, strengthen coping skills, and gain sense of control when in situations of bullying and social rejection.

I need to share with the reader that my approach to bullying is not a simple "ignore it and it will go away" approach. I think it is utterly ridiculous that based on years of research and a duty to humanity we go to great lengths to keep elderly, women, and children safe who suffer domestic violence through creating safety plans and getting them to shelters, but we tell children and adolescents who are being bullied to "just ignore it and the bully will stop." I believe that especially for children and adolescents diagnosed with AS, the more they ignore the bullying the greater the possibility that it could worsen. Attwood (1998) discussed the predatory instinct that can be triggered in peers of the child or adolescent who display the social inadequacies that accompanies AS. I am a firm believer that every child or adolescent who is being bullied needs coping skills to be able to defend themselves, to be empowered to fight back if needed, to be able to get to safety, to know who to go to for help and how to get help, and to be given assistance in repairing the emotional damage that accompanies any form of bullying. I do believe that ignoring is helpful to some degree and must be utilized as part of the approach in dealing with bullying, but it is not "the answer" to making the bullying behavior cease. Children and adolescents diagnosed with AS need help finding a voice with which they can speak up and speak out about what is happening to them when they are being bullied. Children and adolescents who bully often continue to bully peers that appear helpless and who do not retaliate or voice displeasure, somehow believing that it is "O.K" since the bullied child or adolescent did not react. I believe that dealing with bullying must be multidimensional: Helping the child or adolescent mentally, physically, and emotionally; involving the parent regarding the therapist's philosophy and therapy approach in dealing with the bullying; and finally, involving the school or institution in which the bullying is taking place to bring awareness that can result in safety for the child or adolescent on the receiving end of the bullying and providing consequences or interventions for the bully or bullies.

Video Games

I have written in other chapters about my work using video games with children suffering from emotional disturbances, and one of the surprising themes that surfaced for all of the children in the study was that all had encountered bullying and a few were dealing with it at the time of the study (Hull, 2009). There are many themes found in video games that make them useful in the play therapy process when dealing with adolescents diagnosed with AS who are being bullied. The first theme is the release of frustration. Military games and games that contain themes of conquering provide an inner sense of power and an important healthy and safe outlet for emotions. I am well aware of the debate that continues to rage over video games that contain violent content and I always respect parent's wishes when it comes to limiting those types of games for their adolescent. I also respect the age limits that are placed on games to protect younger children from violent content. However, when adolescents describe to me in detail the bullying that they have encountered, images of the Allied soldiers landing on Omaha Beach in World War II come to my mind. I realize that the same mental, emotional, and physical anguish and physiological responses are being triggered in these amazing young people's brains and bodies. I discussed earlier how the overload of negative emotions creates confusion and terror for the child or adolescent diagnosed with AS and can result in them lashing out behaviorally in ways that harm themselves or others and may result in more negative social experiences. Video games can provide a healthy release for the negative emotions and the therapist provides a valuable resource to be able to help the adolescent put their feelings into words through the release that the games can provide.

Another theme that makes computer and video games useful in the play therapy process when dealing with the bullying of an adolescent diagnosed with AS is the sense of control that comes with playing a game. Adolescents diagnosed with AS often share that they feel a sense of safety within the confines of a particular computer or video game, and that they are in charge of the outcome. The complex systems found within many computer and video games mirror the complexities that social situations present to adolescents diagnosed with AS and parallels can be created between the game and real life. One adolescent diagnosed with AS was especially interested in the Sims (Electronic Arts, 2003) video game, a game in which the player creates a person and places the person in various situations and has the ability to create moods and desires for the person. This game provided invaluable material as she and I created parallels between the game and real life in helping her gain valuable social skills as well as understanding the emotions of others. I will discuss further my work using the Sims (Electronic Arts, 2003) in the section dealing with helping adolescents struggling with life's transitions.

A final theme that makes computer and video games useful in the play therapy process with adolescents diagnosed with AS who are being bullied is the working together with another person to reach goals and accomplish tasks. Many individuals diagnosed with AS who are being bullied do not realize that they can reach out to others for assistance. This is because of their inability to put feelings into words or because they don't know how to ask for help. Many of the computer and video games have two-player options that allow for the adolescent and therapist to work together, which provides a model for leaning on someone else in times of emotional and mental distress. I have used several games with the two-player options that allow the adolescent and I to work together, and then I use our connection as a model to help the adolescent understand that it is necessary to rely on others to get through life. Many adolescents diagnosed with AS that I encounter internalize their negative emotions and are either afraid to go to someone to let them know that they are being bullied or it simply does not occur to the adolescent that this is an option. Some adolescents diagnosed with AS believe that adults will not do anything to stop the bullying or that it will bring more attention to the adolescent so they stay silent and suffer in silence, all the while the emotional and mental ravaging goes on inside the adolescent and is undetected by most people around them.

A thirteen-year-old adolescent diagnosed with AS was referred to me because of bullying and the emotional and mental anguish that had occurred as a result of the bullying. He was a lover of the old Super Mario Bros. games and was ecstatic when I revealed my 1988 Nintendo NES console with the original Super Mario Bros. games. I have found that many children and adolescents are drawn to the older games despite the high tech graphics of modern games. For those unfamiliar with the Super Mario Bros. games, there are "bullies" at every turn. Each level has a "boss" that must be defeated to go to the next level, and within each level there are all sorts of "evil" creatures attempting to thwart Mario and Luigi's progress. The player must be watchful as well as be skilled in either getting around these "bullies" or bopping them on the head to defeat them. The most famous "bully" of all, Bowser, awaits as the final impediment in Mario and Luigi's quest of rescuing the elusive princess. Through playing the game, we were able to identify his feelings regarding the bullies, adopt a playful attitude in thinking about the bullies, and also come up with strategies in dealing with the bullies. The game helped lessen the young man's fears and was a factor in helping getting him to speak up and speak out about what was happening to him. I utilized a multidimensional approach in helping this young man and will discuss more about this case in later sections on bullying.

Chess

I discussed the use of chess in working with children diagnosed with AS, and I utilize it in my work with adolescents diagnosed with AS who are struggling with bullying. I find that many of the adolescents diagnosed with AS like the game of chess and there are several components to the game that make it useful to use with the issue of bullying. One component is the use of strategy to outthink one's opponent and capitalize on the opponent's mistakes. A player of average skill can actually do well in chess simply by waiting for the opponent to become careless and capitalize on the opponent's mistake. Or, a player may have a pre-planned design to how they set up the pieces and guide the opponent into a losing situation. The point is that chess is a thinking game, and I apply this idea in my multidimensional approach to bullying in that the adolescent diagnosed with AS who is being bullied needs to know their "opponent" and think out a strategy. The problem is that most children and adolescents who are being bullied simply cannot think; they are in "fight-or-flight" mode and only can react. When the adolescent is finally out of harm's way they do not want to think about the awful experience because it will re-trigger the sympathetic nervous system, so they put it out of their mind as much as possible. I use the game of chess as a metaphor to think out various strategies that can be used against the bully or bullies.

A second component that makes chess useful with adolescents diagnosed with AS who are being bullied is to see things from a different perspective. Chess has a myriad of combinations and options that can cause a chain of events in several different directions. One of the struggles mentioned earlier for individuals diagnosed with AS is mindblindness, which causes a great deal of problems in the individual forming and sustaining relationships. Chess can be a way to help the adolescent diagnosed with AS see a problem from another angle, which can get them to think about someone else's feelings and actions. This is valuable because I have found that when I can help an adolescent diagnosed with AS to begin to understand why someone would continue to bully them (e.g., the bully's lack of self-worth, the teen's apparent apathy toward the bullying, etc.) it can help empower the adolescent to think about other choices rather than allowing it to happen in a learned helplessness manner. I used chess with the thirteen-year-old young man mentioned above as part of the multidimensional approach to get him to think of various strategies that he could implement in dealing with the bully that was bothering him. He mentioned to me that he never thought of the bully being someone who was filled with self-hatred; he only saw the situation through his own lens as a "helpless" victim. This was instrumental in empowering this young man to gain inner strength by utilizing his cognitive abilities.

Physical Activities: Swordfights, Pillow Boxing, and Give your Therapist a Good Shove!

Individuals diagnosed with AS tend to demonstrate "motor clumsiness" (Gillberg, 1991) and often exhibit odd gait and posture. Wing (1981) noted that Asperger himself stated that individuals diagnosed with AS have difficulty with activities involving motor skills such as games and writing and drawing. This clumsiness makes the child and adolescent diagnosed with AS stand out when it comes to activities that involve sports and physical activity. I encountered one young man diagnosed with AS about fourteen years of age who told me that it was actually "painful" for him to run because of the strain on his legs and hips. While his parents were able to provide physical therapy and other treatments to help his physical development, he hated any form of physical activity and dreaded P.E. class at school. I find this to be a common characteristic in children and adolescents diagnosed with AS and these physical difficulties cause them to be the target of teasing, bullying, and social rejection.

I have found that by the time the child reaches adolescence, the motor clumsiness and motor skills deficits have taken a toll on the teen's self-worth and body image, resulting in the adolescent being virtually out of touch with their body. Because many adolescents diagnosed with AS do not enjoy sports due to previous failure or ridicule from peers during their childhood years, they tend to shy away from physical activity and their body becomes a sort of unknown entity, almost separate from themselves. I have observed that many see themselves as unable to fight back and believe that their body has no sort of use other than walking, getting food into their mouths, or playing their beloved computer or video games. The following techniques are part of my multidimensional approach to bullying and get the adolescent diagnosed with AS to practice getting in touch with their bodies and beginning to understand how powerful their physical presence can be. Please note that none of these techniques are designed to encourage the adolescent diagnosed with AS to act out physically against anyone in an unprovoked manner, for that would make the adolescent diagnosed with AS the bully! Instead, these techniques are designed to help the adolescent diagnosed with AS to begin to understand their physical strength and presence which in turn can create an inner power of confidence and self-worth, as well as insulate the adolescent against fear. I recommend that these techniques be implemented only after a solid base of trust and safety are established between the adolescent and the therapist.

Swordfights

I use foam swords that are soft and safe to get the adolescent diagnosed with AS to practice coordinating body movements and muscle groups that are not used very often, and to help them get in touch with their physical presence. If one observes the art of fencing, one will note the grace, elegance, and physical athleticism of the fencers, as well as the agility and speed at which the fencers move. Much like ballroom dancing, it looks easy until one begins to try and imitate what was observed. I share the rules of the game with the adolescent before we begin. The first rule is no blows to the face or head. Even though the swords are soft, the sword could still knock off someone's glasses or poke an eye. If there is a blow to the head or face this is punishable by losing a point. The second rule is that the players must stay in a designated area that is mapped out by the therapist. I have used tape on the floor or moved chairs to make a "ring." The last rule is that any player can call timeout at any time to stop the game when they want to take a break. The players score points when the tip of the sword touches the other player's body (leg, arm, or chest) and the player who reaches the designated amount of points wins the match.

I process the activity with the adolescent after the match, and talk about thoughts and feelings that were elicited from the swordfight. A common reaction during the game is laughter and delight, and most adolescents are surprised by the exhilaration they feel afterwards. I often will go through a "slow motion" match to point out how to defend against an opponent's attack and ways that one's body stance can leave themselves open to an opponent's attack. For instance, an ill-timed power lunge can expose one's back or side. We also work on foot work and stepping aside an attack. I try to get the adolescent to see that one's body is powerful and get them to notice how their hands, feet, and legs all work together in this exercise. The adolescent will usually get more nimble and quick as the matches progress, and I use this to demonstrate how practice increases motor skills and introduce the thought that physical activity can be fun. The adolescent also experiences using their body in a new way and this can help with self-worth and improving body image.

Pillow Boxing

Pillow boxing is a fun activity that involves one person holding a pillow while the other person punches it. I use couch pillows and hold them by the corners with my arms fully outstretched and instruct the adolescent to punch the pillow as hard as they can. I find that many adolescents diagnosed with AS find this absurd at first, but after a few punches begin to enjoy it. I instruct them to alternate between the left and right hands when throwing the punches in order to work both sides of the body. I encourage them while holding the pillow, saying "That's it! Good Job!" The purpose of this exercise is to release frustration as well as being able to get the adolescent into a physical activity that uses parts of their bodies in a new way. This helps to stimulate their reflexes and also forces them to think about their bodies and connect this thinking with the feeling of movement and control.

I encounter many adolescents diagnosed with AS that have great anger towards the bully or bullies and some share their fantasies of inflicting physical harm on the person or persons. I allow them to vent these thoughts and feelings and while I discuss the consequences of physically taking revenge on these individuals, I encourage the adolescent to put these feelings into words. I always end these sessions by addressing the adolescent's intent after the venting; making sure that there is no real intent to harm anyone. This activity is a good physical release of frustration and I have witnessed some adolescents diagnosed with AS that burst into tears as they get into a frenzied rhythm of punching. When this occurs I spend time processing the emotional release and helping to explain where the reaction comes from and that it is normal for our bodies to want to get rid of the stress that so many people carry. I work to normalize the experience and provide a sense of safety for the adolescent that helps to not leave them more traumatized following the emotional release. Many children and adolescents diagnosed with AS internalize feelings and then "blow," causing harm to themselves or others, damaging property, and receiving negative consequences that leaves them even more confused by their emotions and their physical reaction. Pillow boxing provides a healthy, controlled, physical and emotional release that I believe many individuals who internalize emotions need. Pillow boxing represents part of the multidimensional approach that I use for bullying in that there may be a time when the child or adolescent needs to use their fists to get away from the bully and protect themselves until help can come. By practicing boxing in this safe and fun way, the adolescent gains awareness of their body and the power that one's body can generate, leading the way to inner confidence and positive beliefs about oneself.

Give Your Therapist A Good Shove!

I must give credit for this approach to my older brothers, who would tease me by taking a favorite toy and hiding it behind them, daring me to "come and get it." I would slam into them trying desperately to get my beloved toy, but they being much older and bigger would simply sling me away from them and I would careen into the grass or couch. I loved it! While I do not inflict any harm on my clients, I use the approach to get them to experience physical contact with another person and to feel the force that they can generate with their body against another person. Again, the idea of this activity is to create awareness for the adolescent diagnosed with AS so they get the idea that their physical presence is powerful and to allow them to feel a sense of power that is connected to their bodies.

I begin the activity by getting the adolescent to look at how they normally stand. I have observed that many adolescents diagnosed with AS often display poor posture and slouching that may be related to the motor clumsiness and lack of body awareness. I then have them role-play what happens to their body when the bully or bullies approach them, and usually the adolescent will show me a wilted posture that appears defenseless and weak. I role-play along with the adolescent, and I am careful to ensure that the adolescent knows that I am not making fun of them, but that our bodies can have odd appearances at times. I then tell them about the puffer fish and how it can blow itself up and ward off enemies simply by growing several times its size. I then show them a power stance in which I place my feet shoulder-width apart, stretch my body as tall as I can, square my shoulders, and place my hands on my hips. We role play this back and forth and I make the connection that when a person stands in their power stance, a message is sent that says, "I am strong. I am confident. I am ready for anything."

I then take an object such as a stuffed animal, hacky sack, or a fossil egg and place it behind me on my desk and I tell them that they must get that object. I tell them that I am not going to hurt them but that I am going to block them and they will need to shove past me in order to get the object. The adolescent is usually timid at first, as this is *not* everyday behavior even for a neurotypical individual. The first time that the adolescent tries to get by me I resist only slightly, and I turn my body away from them and keeping my hands and arms at my side to help them get the object. As time goes on the adolescent becomes a bit bolder and slides past me fairly easily. I then tell them that I am going to become more resistant, but I reassure them that I am not going to hurt them. This time I place my feet further apart and "puff" up and lean into them as they try to get past. I tell them, "Push! Try harder! You have to get past me! Shove me out of the way!" They usually are giggling and sometimes frustrated at this point, but most are successful in getting me out of the way. This goes on for a few repetitions until the adolescent feels comfortable and confident getting past me. I then share with them that I am going to become even more resistant but again reassure them that I am not going to hurt them. I remind them that it is OK to shove me as hard as they want to get the object. I use my arms slightly at this level, leaning into the adolescent and moving my feet to block their progress. When I feel them exerting more force than they have in the previous two rounds, I ease up and let them get the object, praising them for their bravery and effort. I encourage them, cheer them, and then we process their thoughts and feelings about the activity.

I use this activity to bring into the teen's awareness that they have strength and power. At the time of this writing I am 6'1" and 225 pounds. I share with the adolescent that if they can get me out of the way, they are probably going to be able to get past the people they encounter in middle and high school. These activities that I have presented help demystify the thought of battling, punching, and shoving another person. I speak with many adolescents who are being bullied who share with me that their "worst fear" is being hit or punched. I tell them that NFL players are afraid each game until they get that first hit out of the way; and boxers rejoice when they can take that first punch, realize they are not going to die from it, and get to the business of boxing. Following these activities, many tell me that they are not as afraid of being punched or being hit, realizing that while it might hurt, the adolescent is not going to die from it. For many who are suffering from bullying the actual fear is the fear of the unknown, the fear of what the bully *might* do. I help them see through these activities that their physical presence has power and that they have a "force" within them that can manifest itself through their physical bodies.

I utilized all three of these physical activity approaches with the thirteen-year-old man that I mentioned earlier. He gained a greater sense of the power in his body, which in turn provided him with a much stronger self-worth and an inner sense of safety. He told me proudly, "The kid bullying me isn't even half as big as you, and I moved you pretty easy!" His mother reported that the tantrums that had begun in order to avoid school ceased and he was talkative again on the way to and from school. This young man benefitted from being able to see himself in a new way. Instead of seeing himself as helpless and weak, he began to be aware of his physical strength as well as his mental ability to strategize solutions. Through a multidimensional approach, this young man learned valuable lessons about himself that hopefully will generalize as he continues to move through life's transitions.

PLAY THERAPY TO HELP THE ADOLESCENT DIAGNOSED WITH ASPERGER'S SYNDROME IMPROVE SOCIAL SKILLS

Adolescents diagnosed with AS usually struggle with social skills. Social-skills deficits are the result of a myriad of issues that I have discussed earlier. Thus, my approach to helping adolescents diagnosed with AS gain better social skills is a multidimensional approach that involves a blend of techniques that are directed toward developing cognitive awareness and emotional understanding in the young person. Mindblindness and alexithymia are two of the main problems that contribute to the social difficulties of individuals diagnosed with AS. Adolescents diagnosed with AS can often appear out of place and oblivious to the social structure around them, despite the fact that the adolescent looks the same as peers in physical growth and development. The following techniques provide a multidimensional approach to helping the adolescent diagnosed with AS experience social relationships through the connection with the therapist and group experiences, as well as helping the adolescent better understand their own emotions and the emotions of others, and helping the adolescent learn to see situations from a different perspective.

Game Play

Game play involves any game that the therapist wishes to use such as board games, card games, or strategy games. I have a very simple Tic-Tac-Toe game made of wood with blue and white marbles that is a wonderful conversation starter and begins the process of building the therapeutic relationship. Games that are familiar help to reduce the adolescent's defenses and also allow the modeling of the start of a relationship. Those who work with adolescents diagnosed with AS know that these young people often desire relationships with others but do not know how to go about beginning a friendship (Attwood, 1998; Bromfield, 2010). I have encountered adolescents diagnosed with AS who have asked me "How do I make a friend?" and I have responded with the question "How did our relationship begin?" We then review the dynamics of how the relationship started, how we talked about things that interested us, and how we joined in playing games that we both enjoy. This lays a valuable foundation for examining more complex interactional dynamics such as joint attention and verbal responses that indicate interest. The relationship with the therapist can be a powerful prototype from which the intricate details of the therapeutic relationship can be generalized to other relationships that the adolescent will have the opportunity to build. Game play gets this process started and throughout game play there is the opportunity to build on the levels of trust, respect, and safety that are put in place by spending time together through playing a game.

I met with a young man about seventeen years old diagnosed with AS who desperately wanted a close friend. It was as if he had "woken up" from a deep sleep and suddenly felt an intense need for closeness. He had formed several "online" friendships through an online game he regularly played, and through this positive experience decided it was time to find a "real-live friend" but told me how he was "so lonely" and felt "isolated." This new desire frightened him but intrigued him at the same time. It is not uncommon for adolescents diagnosed with AS to appear to be delayed in sexual and social development, however, research shows that puberty occurs at normal rates in individuals diagnosed with AS but development is hampered by social and emotional deficits (Hénault & Attwood, 2005). For these adolescents, it is as if the awareness of a sexual desire and social relationships changes from something that is abstract and intangible to something this is real and able to be grasped. This young man definitely was experiencing many feelings and desires all at once, and many of our sessions of sifting through his feelings and thoughts felt like we were sifting through random objects that I knew had some meaning but the final answer to all of this "stuff" was not clear. He was discouraged because in his opinion his previous attempts to secure a friend had failed. He explained more about this and I realized that his eagerness to make a friendship was having the opposite effect on people and appeared to have pushed people away.

During our sessions we played a homemade board game called "Wahoo" that has been in my family for generations, and this young man liked this game very much. The game is similar to "Aggravation" and uses marbles and dice that are rolled to help move each player's marbles around the board until the entire player's marbles are all safe at the "home" base. I use the game to illustrate that in life one has choices based on the circumstances that one encounters in daily life. The number that comes up on the dice is something that I cannot control; however, I have several choices that I can make that will have a direct impact on the outcome of the game. I used this to help the young man understand that one cannot simply "make" a friendship, like going to pick out a new car or buying new clothes. I mapped out how patience, timing, and technique are factors in the building of a relationship. I used our relationship in this process as a reference point and we dissected the process of our building a friendship through playing the game. Two things that were an impediment to this young man were impatience and intensity. The game provided a wonderful way to demonstrate patience because a player is at the mercy of the dice and can only move as far as the number on the dice. I was able to use the game to work on intensity by teaching the young man how our relationship grew gradually and that much like the game, there is a progression that follows order and structure. By having a picture of a relationship and walking through the steps of how it was formed through playing this game, this young man was better prepared to make friends, and I am proud to say that he was able to!

Group Play

I discussed the power of group play and how it can be utilized to help children diagnosed with AS improve social skills. Group play is very useful with adolescents diagnosed with AS and I have found group work to be a wonderful practice ground to teach practical skills in a fun and relaxed manner. The group experience allows adolescents diagnosed with AS to come in contact with others who have the same struggles, interests, and gifts. Group interaction allows each member's gifts, talents, and interests to be celebrated in an open forum. I have found that many adolescents diagnosed with AS often get pushed aside in large groups because many feel intimidated and struggle with communicating thoughts and ideas in an environment that their brains interpret as threatening. A small group is more controlled and less threatening for most adolescents diagnosed with AS and research supports the efficacy of group work for the teaching of social skills (Epp, 2008; Neufeld and Wolfberg, 2010). There are many games that can be utilized in group play such as card games, strategy games, and board games. Group activities such as putting a puzzle together is also helpful, and art projects or building something as a group is another way of getting the adolescent diagnosed with AS to become comfortable with a group and to be able to observe others and interact. There are three techniques that I use in my group work that help with social skills: (1) the Talking, Feeling, Doing Game (Gardner, 1973); (2) the Pez Game; and (3) role-playing various social situations such as ordering food at a restaurant. I will briefly discuss each of these and how I utilize them in group play.

The Talking, Feeling, Doing Game

The Talking, Feeling, Doing Game (Gardner, 1973) is a popular game that is used in therapy with children and adolescents. Gardner (1973) originally designed the game for children and adolescents that were resistant to the therapy process. I use the game in my social-skills groups with adolescents diagnosed with AS because the game provides a fun activity that brings connection among group members, but it also gets group members to talk about their thoughts and feelings related to various situations as well as incorporating the physical acting out of certain behaviors. I have found this game is a tool for breaking down the barriers that mindblindness and alexithymia create, through gentleness and in a non-threatening way, helping each group member practice hearing another's response and viewing it from a different perspective and working to understand another's emotions. The Talking and Feeling cards are especially good for getting an adolescent to practice sharing emotions and ideas in a group setting, and the group as a whole has the opportunity to dissect the scenario presented on the card with each member sharing their thoughts and feelings. I listen carefully to each response and use the scenario presented on the card to use it as a social-skills teaching opportunity.

For example, some of the cards bring up a scenario and then ask the question "What is the boy or girl thinking?" This sometimes elicits frustration from some of the group members because of the vague and abstract nature of the question and it veers the adolescent away from the typical logic-only approach that many individuals diagnosed with AS exhibit, forcing them to shift to a new dimension. I challenge them to "imagine" what might someone being bullied be thinking or feeling and to "pretend you are in their shoes." It is amazing to see how most of the adolescents diagnosed with AS are able to gradually make this shift. I believe that individuals diagnosed with AS can learn to see things from another's perspective as well as understand other's emotions, but they need to be taught how to do this and then practice doing it. The group experience provides this and reinforces the concepts for generalization to other situations.

The Pez Game

I have several Pez candy dispensers displayed in my office. The characters that I have range from Disney characters like the Toy Story crew to Superheroes like Spiderman and The Incredible Hulk. It dawned on me one day while searching for metaphors that each Pez dispenser character represents a different personality and temperament, and also represents different individual talents and abilities. The "Pez Game" involves giving each group member a different Pez dispenser and the group member must take on the character qualities of the Pez dispenser that they are given. For example, an adolescent may be given Shrek. Shrek is a bit grumpy and is easily annoyed, and is very proud of being an ogre. The adolescent would be instructed to "be Shrek" and act out those characteristics that Shrek exhibits. Then the adolescent pretending to be Shrek would be instructed to interact with the adolescent holding the Buzz Lightyear Pez dispenser, who would take on the characteristics of Buzz. Through pretending to adopt other character's personalities and temperaments, the adolescent practices role-playing by being someone else and pretending to experience how that person would think and feel, which is important in helping the adolescent gain skills that help lessen the effects of mindblindness and alexithymia.

Some adolescents diagnosed with AS are very hesitant to join in this game and can appear confused or irritated with the request. I am cautious to not push an adolescent diagnosed with AS into an activity that raises their anxiety too high. I am grateful for any adolescent diagnosed with AS just to be in the group in the first place. I have found that even the most resistant will eventually join in at some point. I gently invite them into the activity, but if I sense that they are overwhelmed or they tell me outright that they do not want to participate, I reassure them that it is OK and say, "That is fine _____, when you are ready just let me know." I then move on to the next group member and encourage them to take their turn, and I always join in to get things started and model the idea of the activity for the group members. The therapist must remember that some group activities may trigger fear in group members and I am a firm believer in showing empathy and respect for every member. I stay non-reactive and never interpret an adolescent's silence or resistance as a defiant gesture; furthermore, I use it to model gentleness, kindness, and patience.

Role-Playing Social Situations

The group-play experience allows children and adolescents diagnosed with AS to watch, learn, and practice social skills in a fun and relaxed manner. I am a proponent of giving children and adolescents diagnosed with AS the opportunity to practice social skills in the hopes that what is learned in the group will generalize to other social settings. The role-playing activity begins with each member randomly drawing a note card from a basket on which I have written a scenario such as ordering food at a fast-food restaurant, meeting someone for the first time and introducing oneself, or asking for directions when one is lost. The player can either read the card out loud and then role-play the situation or they can say "pass" and select another card out of the basket to role-play. The group members earn chips (plastic tokens) for a successful role-play: If the group member role-plays the scenario, they receive two chips; if they pass and successfully role-play the second card, the group member can earn one chip; if a group member does not want to attempt a scenario at all and another group member successful takes that member's role-play they can earn three chips. A role-play is considered successful simply by the group member attempting to perform the role-play. I use each scenario as an opportunity to teach and model social skills for the group and to invite group discussion regarding the scenario.

PLAY THERAPY TO HELP WITH EMOTIONAL REGULATION AND EMOTIONAL IMMATURITY

I discussed in Chapter Six how the physical, cognitive, and emotional development of the individual diagnosed with AS is asynchronous in nature. The goal of therapists who work with children, adolescents, and adults diagnosed with AS is to pull them up the developmental ladder as much as possible. This is a daunting task. I would love to be able to tell you that I go home each evening very happy and encouraged and that *all* of the young people diagnosed with AS that I work with are making developmental leaps and that their families are completely healthy and satisfied with the progress that their child or adolescent has made. Sadly, I cannot say that. I do want the reader to know that the progress that I have shared in the cases in this book is absolutely true, but there are setbacks in working with this population. For every monumental success in one case, there are setbacks in five others. A therapist who is going to work with this population and attempt to help pull children and adolescents diagnosed with AS up the developmental ladder must know and remember that the work can be arduous and the progress can be slow.

The following play therapy techniques are designed to help the therapist in creating synchrony in the adolescent diagnosed with AS, and these techniques are part of the multidimensional process of helping with overall social-skill deficits. These techniques specifically address the emotional issues of the adolescent diagnosed with AS that causes disruptions in the building and sustaining of relationships.

Computer and Video Games

I have discussed the use of video games as a play-therapy tool throughout the book and I have found that computer and video games prove to be useful in helping an adolescent diagnosed with AS learn to regulate emotion. Computer and video games have a common theme in that to be successful in a game one must play with a sense of control and follow the rules. This concept provides a metaphor for regulating emotions in that one must be in control to regulate emotion. I use the games to introduce this concept and gradually help the adolescent diagnosed with AS to understand and utilize this concept. One way to do this is to put the adolescent in a situation where they feel out of control. I accomplish this by finding a game that the adolescent has never played before and put the game on the hardest level and allow the adolescent to fail. Many adolescents resort to pushing all of the buttons at once, which usually makes things worse. After a few minutes, the adolescent is frustrated from feeling out of control and gives up.

I then walk through the experience with the adolescent and process thoughts and feelings. Dissecting thoughts and feelings can take some time with individuals diagnosed with AS so the therapist needs to be patient during this phase. I find it helpful to videotape the game playing experience to review it later because this can be paused and rewound several times in order to get the adolescent to remember how they felt and identify what they were thinking during the experience. It is also important to get the adolescent to identify what they feel in their bodies in addition to feelings and thoughts. Most talk about feelings such as anger, fear, frustration, and say things like, "My hands got really sweaty" or "I started breathing really hard" or "I hate this game, it is making me really mad." I use this to introduce the physiological response of the sympathetic nervous system and the fight-or-flight response. At this point, relaxation techniques can be implemented to help the adolescent learn to lessen the effects of the physiological response in order to give them tools that keep them grounded. I have devised a checklist that the adolescent and I go over to demonstrate how positive thoughts can also ground a person to stay in control. Some of these items on the checklist are

"Am I going to die if I don't do well in this game?" and "What is the worst that can happen if I don't complete this level?" I help them understand that the fight-or-flight process that stirs up emotions can make someone feel as though they are in some sort of danger, but the truth is that most of the time there is no danger. I believe that helping adolescents diagnosed with AS understand the fight-or-flight process and how their brain and body respond is very important in helping them learn to not only regulate emotion but to face difficult social situations as well as life's transitions.

I instruct the adolescent play the level again at the same level of difficulty but instead using the tools that I have given them. We then review the adolescent's experience and reprocess the thoughts and feelings. By going over this sequence repeatedly, the adolescent is able to practice experiencing negative emotions but keeping themselves calm. I introduce other games that the adolescent has not played and we go over the same routine. The goal of this technique is that the skills learned from practicing controlling emotions through playing the games will generalize to other situations like home or school. Many adolescents diagnosed with AS discover that they are better able to play the game and concentrate when they stay relaxed and feel more in control, which I then build upon to give them a reference point that they can think more clearly when they are in control of their emotions. This technique is powerful in that many of the struggles that individuals diagnosed with AS encounter are related to them becoming overwhelmed by their emotions, and this allows the adolescent to practice self-soothing when they are becoming frustrated.

A thirteen-year-old young man in the sixth grade diagnosed with AS was referred to me for issues with being unable to control his emotions. He would tantrum like a four-year-old over seemingly insignificant things, which led to problems at school and created difficulties at home with his younger siblings. He was typical of young people who struggle with emotional regulation in that when he was calm and rational he knew that his behavior was not appropriate and he even expressed feelings of remorse over his behavior, but in the heat of the emotional upheaval, he was unable to control himself. I used the game Tetris that we played on the original Nintendo NES. I allowed him to show me his skills and he did fairly well on level one and two. I then put the game on level fifteen and the pieces began to fall very quickly and he was unable to clear one line. I reset the level and the scenario was repeated. The third time the young man became visibly frustrated when the pieces fell into a jumbled pile and he failed to clear even one line. We processed his thoughts, feelings, and bodily sensations in the manner that I described above. Through slowing things down, I was able to help him identify his emotions and thought processes that let to him getting frustrated. This young man enjoyed science and liked learning about the human body and the role of the sympathetic nervous system, and we even drew a brain and labeled the parts. Gradually, he was able to become more and more aware of when he began to "ramp up" and was able to lessen his reactions before completely losing control. While the tantrums did not completely cease immediately, they lessened in frequency and duration. I am convinced that as this young man's cognitive and emotional development continues, his ability to better regulate his emotions will continue.

PLAY THERAPY TO HELP WITH THE TRANSITIONS OF LIFE

Adolescents diagnosed with AS encounter several transitional points along the path of adolescence that can create emotional, psychological, and social problems. The final transitional point, adulthood, looms like a dark, giant mountain with many unknown paths and challenges. I encounter several young adults diagnosed with AS who struggle with the transition from adolescence to adulthood. Some are gripped with fear, others by self-doubt, and I work very hard to help them see that most people enter the adulthood phase feeling the same way but I try to empower them to gain skills in order to reach their full potential. I discussed in Chapter Six the important role that support plays for those diagnosed with AS who are moving into adulthood. I have found that with guidance, encouragement, and sometimes a gentle nudge, these amazing individuals find their niche and are able to follow their dreams. The techniques discussed in this section are designed to get the adolescent diagnosed with AS to begin thinking about adulthood and to gradually break down the fear and self-doubt so that the adolescent begins to see the opportunities that adulthood brings, as well as give them a positive, strength-based view of themselves and the future.

The SIMS Game

Fanning and Brighton (2007) explored the use of the Sims2 as a therapeutic tool and found positive responses from therapists who believe that the game would be useful in therapy with children and adolescents. Skigen (2008) has written a wonderful chapter on the usefulness of the Sims computer game in play therapy with children and adolescents. I too have found the game useful in helping to understand how an adolescent sees their world, such as which parts of the world are important to the adolescent and which parts are not, and to how the adolescent views relationships. A fascinating facet of the game is that players create their Sim, a representation of themselves complete with personality, marital history, and job skills. The player can choose from five game modes that allow for different game experiences. For instance, Live mode is where the current action is taking place, Buy mode is used when the player needs to purchase something, Build mode is when the player is creating something, and Camera mode allows the player to record what has happened. The player is in complete control of all the aspects of their Sim's life, including meeting and interacting with others, going to a job, and even sleeping. There are many versions of the SIMS game that have different themes, but the main premise is the same: The player builds their Sim and creates a fictitious world for their Sim, controlling the day to day activities of their Sim and providing for its needs that mirror real life. In the Options mode, a player can choose "Free Will" for their Sim in which the Sim takes on different moods and attitudes and makes choices "on their own" apart from the player's control.

The Sims games have several advantages for work with adolescents diagnosed with AS, from opening up discussion regarding emotions, social interactions, and finding what needs are important to the adolescent, but it also works well with those facing transitions. The Sims world can become quite chaotic at times, just like the real world. This provides an opportunity for the adolescent to practice decision-making skills and finding balance through prioritizing and organization. The creation of a Sim and the building of that Sim's world provide an outlet for working through subconscious fears and facing those fears and allow the therapist to gain insight into the thought process of an adolescent facing a difficult transition.

I used the Sims game with an adolescent diagnosed with AS who was struggling with transitioning to a new school following a move from another region of the state. Not only was everything unfamiliar, but there were challenges of a bigger school and a larger community. The Sims game allowed the adolescent to create a world that resembled where he had lived before prior to the move and gave me insight into what the adolescent valued in his prior environment. We were able to find similarities between his previous environment and his new one. One day when we were playing the game I encouraged him to try changing some of the familiar areas in which his Sim lived. While resistant at first, he added one building and then another. We then talked about his feelings and what bothered him about new places. Through game play, we were able to examine his fears and thoughts about change and introduce the theme of facing those fears, and he began to adjust much better at school and told me that he felt more comfortable in his new place but added, "I still miss where I used to live."

The Game of LIFE

The game of LIFE is a useful game to play with adolescents diagnosed with AS who are approaching adulthood. The themes of facing college, managing money, choosing a career, buying a house, etc. are all embedded in the game and get the adolescent to examine the challenges and opportunities that adulthood brings. Regardless of whether I am working with neurotypical individuals or adolescents diagnosed with AS, I emphasize the positive characteristics that adulthood brings: Freedom, new avenues of learning, and self-discovery that leads to joy. I am bothered by adults who preach to adolescents about how hard life is and the treacherous, overwhelming, and insurmountable challenges that await them in adulthood. No wonder our adolescents find entering the "real world" intimidating and approach this transition with timidity. Adulthood has its challenges and the world can be scary at times, but adolescents must be given encouragement that leads to a positive outlook and strengthening of resolve.

I used the game of LIFE with a young man diagnosed with AS who was approaching his senior year of high school. Like many young people diagnosed with AS, his IQ was very high and he had done very well academically, which had brought invitations from several universities and colleges. His parents were encouraging him going to college, but he was quite resistant. Through playing the game of LIFE, the young man was able to face some of his fears and he revealed to me his great fear of "failure." We examined his thinking that related to this fear, and he categorized his thoughts about failure in a black-and-white, all-or-nothing manner. The game was instrumental in helping him shift away from this type of thinking and gain a different perspective. For example, the game of LIFE helped him see that being laid off from a job and transitioning to another career is not failing but a challenge that must be addressed. A major house repair that costs a lot of money is a challenge that can be addressed through several different avenues but it is not failure. Over time, this young man gradually became ready to face the fears of transitioning to college and adulthood and playing the game of LIFE was very helpful in this process.

PLAY THERAPY TO HELP FAMILIES OF ADOLESCENTS DIAGNOSED WITH ASPERGER'S SYNDROME DEAL WITH STRESS AND CHALLENGES

I have shared throughout the book how families of children and adolescents diagnosed with AS experience great deals of stress, sadness, disappointments, and daily challenges. Part of the passion that I have in helping children and adolescents diagnosed with AS is directed at helping the families of these remarkable young people and cheering the parents and caregivers on in their quest to love their children and help them. Encouragement and hope are vital ingredients in keeping these parents and caregivers motivated to keep striving because I firmly believe that a parent or caregiver's discouragement is passed on to the child or adolescent diagnosed with AS. Part of helping these parents and caregivers is reminding them to see the blessings of their children and adolescents and to celebrate victories however small they seem, and to continue to see their children and adolescents diagnosed with AS in light of their gifts, talents, and abilities. I spoke with a mother recently who put it so well: "My son has AS, but AS does not have him!"

The techniques with the families of adolescents diagnosed with AS are similar to those that are described in Chapter Five. Getting the family to play a game together in the therapy office helps to build connection, increase communication, and help the parents, caregivers, and siblings of the adolescent diagnosed with AS see the adolescent in a new light. A family art project allows the family to work together to create something, and in doing so the family can vent out frustration, laugh, cry, and connect on a much deeper level. Prescribing families to play together on a regular basis at home helps reduce the effects of stress and build coping skills among the individual members as well as coping skills for the family unit. Siblings of adolescents diagnosed with AS often feel left out of families and playing together can help reconnect the siblings in a new way with their sibling diagnosed with AS.

I worked with a family of four comprised of a mother, father, and two children. The oldest boy was about fifteen and was diagnosed with AS, and his younger sister was about twelve. This family was not in crisis by any means, but there was some distance beginning to occur as the younger sibling was gifted in music and athletics and had activities each weekend. The mother noticed some resentment in the young man diagnosed with AS, and he had begun lashing out verbally and with mild physical behavior toward his sister which prompted the mother to bring him to counseling. I worked with him individually each week, and I scheduled family sessions about every third week. During the family sessions we played "Wahoo," the game that I mentioned earlier in the chapter. The game brought out themes of intense competition between the two siblings and opened up good dialogue among the family about the brewing conflict between brother and sister. The father revealed that he saw what was going on between the two but did not know how to handle it, and the mother played the role of peacemaker or referee. During my individual sessions with the young man, I helped uncover his resentment toward his sister and helped him put his thoughts and feelings into words. He shared with me that he saw her as "perfect" and felt as though his parents favored her. However, he was also able to see that he rarely voiced his feelings about her nor did he voice his desires of wanting his parents to do more with him. We worked on helping him find his voice within the family and the family sessions helped to provide a practice ground for him to share his thoughts and feelings in the safety of the therapy office and with me there to assist him. The family had no idea that he was feeling neglected and rejected, and his younger sister shared with him with tears in her eyes how much she loved him and felt that every time she tried to get close to him she felt as though he pushed her away. Through this sharing, there was a pathway to deeper connection, better communication, and bonding as a family unit. I think of this family often because it encourages me to meet with families and never to neglect the family unit. Had I continued to meet with just the young man, this underlying current of feelings of rejection could potentially have grown into quite a problem down the road in his development.

A CASE STUDY

The Case of Jason: Play Therapy with an Adolescent Diagnosed with Asperger's Syndrome

Jason was a thirteen-year-old Caucasian male referred to me by his parents for therapy to help prepare him to return to regular school after being home-schooled for two years. His parents stated that due to financial constraints and Jason's high IQ, home-schooling was no longer an option. Jason had been misdiagnosed as a child, which is not uncommon for children and adolescents diagnosed with AS, and this had caused him and his parents a great deal of grief. Throughout his childhood he was labeled ADHD, Oppositional Defiant, and finally Bipolar and placed on all sorts of medications that did nothing for him other than cause a great deal of anxiety and depression, which produced physical manifestations such as scratching and picking at himself. While a discussion of misdiagnosis and over-medication is outside the scope of this book, I will say that many children and adolescents diagnosed with AS are often labeled with the ADHD and Oppositional Defiant labels and placed on many unnecessary medications. Jason's parents decided to remove him from school and home-school him because of the problems that Jason was experiencing at school, which consisted of social isolation by peers and self-injurious behavior as well as academic issues. By the time his parents decided to home-school him, Jason had buried himself deep inside himself and trusted no one but his parents and had begun to shy away from all social situations. Thankfully, they found a psychiatrist who was able to correctly diagnose Jason with AS and took him off all the medications that he had previously been on and placed him on a mild anti-anxiety medication. Soon, the behaviors of picking and scratching ceased. His parents shared his history and told me that Jason had a very high IQ and loved to read, study nature and animals, and enjoyed the outdoors.

Jason was the young man whom I mentioned earlier in Chapter Three, when discussing being comfortable with silence, who would not speak to me until I finally learned to shut up and "just be." Our walks (or runs) around the lake became our whole sessions as he would bound up to a tree, share some scientific fact with me about the tree, and then dart over to a bush and quickly show me where a snake had been laying not long before. I raced to keep up with him, absorbing all of it. At night following the sessions I would look up some of the information he shared and jot down some notes so I did not forget what he told me. Jason was an encyclopedia! I noticed that gradually he did not go so fast, and every now and then he would answer a question if I asked him something about his childhood. During our sessions I kept having to fight my traditional, box-like training that estimated if I was making progress, or questioning if I was wasting time by being outside on our walks. I consciously made an effort to dump this thinking and focus back to Jason, observing his gait, his speaking patterns, and his shining eyes that sparkled when he focused on a bird, insect, or tree. I found myself telling my family many of the facts that Jason shared with me, and one day at lunch with a colleague I found myself excitedly telling him about the egg-laying cycle of the monarch butterfly. Needless to say, this young man made a powerful impression on me.

Suddenly, our walks by the lake ceased. Jason simply sat on the couch in my office one afternoon and said that he did not want to go. He saw my chess game and said, "Let's play chess." We set up the chess game and began to play. While I knew that he was very bright, I had no idea he was a chess master. He quickly demolished me and was obviously delighted because his eyes danced, twinkling back at me and he smiled a devilish grin. "Set 'em back up" he said, and we proceeded to play again. This time I did better, but all I could do was hold on and watch my dissemination unfold before my eyes. "One more time," he said, glancing at my clock. I could see he loved this. Our third game went a bit longer, I am proud to say, but I was soundly beaten. "Let's play chess next time," he said as he got up and walked out of the room. That evening on the way home I pondered why Jason had suddenly stopped our walks and wanted to stay inside the office and play chess. I hoped it was because he had finally begun to trust me more and was willing to sit and be in an enclosed area with me. It turns out I was right.

An amazing transformation happened as we shifted from our outside activities to playing chess. Jason began to share things from within himself, instead of things about himself. I realized that the walks and the sharing of nature and looking at insects, reptiles, animals, and trees were simply a sliver of who he was. He shared details of those days in kindergarten, when the other children stared at him. He shared intimate details of first grade, second grade, and so on when he felt like he was "coming out of his skin." His memory was sharp and clear, and he talked of feeling like dying and not wanting to be him. The feelings poured from him and I restrained myself from giving any form of interpretation, judgment, or response other than empathy and letting him know I heard him and that I was glad that he felt safe enough to tell me. It made sense why he did not want to go back to regular school. For Jason, it was like a concentration camp, not so much because of the social rejection but because of how bad he was feeling. He told me that the game of chess helped him talk about his past pain because it helped him feel comfortable.

I used the game of chess as a way to work on Jason's fears about school and returning and readjusting to a setting that was traumatic for him. He loved the game so much and was so knowledgeable about the game, that it was fairly easy to pull metaphors from the game. I used the metaphor of how each game of chess is different to represent how his return to school would be different. Jason was in a much better place than he was before when he was in school, and he would not be returning to the same school. I also used the metaphor of the interactive pieces of chess and how each piece has its own unique function and ability, to represent how Jason had his own unique abilities, gifts, and interests. This was useful to help increase Jason's sense of self-worth. The other metaphor that was useful was to help Jason see situations from another perspective. One of the things that made Jason such a good chess player was his ability to look at the board and view the game from several different angles. This was helpful in examining Jason's fears from several different vantage points.

The case of Jason turned out to be very successful. He was able to go back to regular school and did well. I continued to see him over the next four years through middle school and high school. Jason had challenges along the way with social skills and adjusting to the various transitional challenges that growing up entails. But his self-worth stayed intact and continued to increase. I became a much better chess player because of Jason and I became a much better therapist because of him. He taught me to be patient, to listen to understand, and to "just be." Today, Jason is in college and has plans to help children who have struggles much like he did. I believe that he is going to do amazing things with his life.

Chapter 8

Divorce and Grief and Loss Issues

OVERVIEW

Divorce and grief/loss are two common issues that prompt parents to bring children and adolescents for therapy. Children and adolescents diagnosed with AS are not immune to the effects of divorce and grief/loss, and any child or adolescent with special needs requires specialized therapeutic approaches to deal with these issues. I have found that children and adolescents diagnosed with AS have special struggles, and the issues that arise from divorce and grief/loss affect them in several unique ways. I wanted to include a special chapter that helps therapists working with children and adolescents diagnosed with AS who are struggling with divorce and grief/loss to identify the special needs of these remarkable young people and introduce play therapy techniques that can be utilized in powerful and effective ways.

DIVORCE AND CHILDREN AND ADOLESCENTS DIAGNOSED WITH ASPERGER'S SYNDROME

Divorce represents a catastrophic upheaval in a family system. Literature abounds on the increase in the divorce rate in our culture and much research has been done on the effects of divorce on children and adolescents (Ahrons, 2007). While I agree that divorce is devastating for all involved, it appears to have become a fixed part of our culture and therapists who work with children and adolescents must be armed with techniques to help empower these young people to weather the storms that inevitably accompany divorce.

Ahrons (2007; 2010) presents an empowering strength-based view of divorce, stating that children and adolescents can learn from the experience as well as gain important strengths and coping skills because of the experience. I like this approach because it helps to reduce learned helplessness and the victim mentality in young people. Therapy in this model provides a safe place for a child or adolescent to release thoughts and emotion and go through the grieving process, but it also helps to provide coping skills which lead to strengthening the young person emotionally and cognitively and preparing them to face future challenges.

EFFECTS OF DIVORCE ON THE CHILD OR ADOLESCENT DIAGNOSED WITH ASPERGER'S SYNDROME

Emotional Effects

I have written previously about the emotional challenges that the child or adolescent diagnosed with AS faces. Emotional regulation difficulties, emotional immaturity, fears, and alexithymia are just a few of the emotional issues that children and adolescents diagnosed with AS contend with. Many children and adolescents diagnosed with AS attempt to deal with fear through clinging to routines that allow them to feel a sense of control over the world around them. Divorce disrupts these routines and affects the child or adolescent emotionally by stirring up fears and creating insecurity. I discussed how the child and adolescent diagnosed with AS has difficulty understanding their own emotions and the emotions of others (alexithymia) and how the emotional upheaval that divorce triggers causes intense withdrawn behavior. The inability to put emotions into words represents yet another challenge for the child or adolescent diagnosed with AS, and compounds the effects of the divorce that can create a verbal shutdown in the child or adolescent who already has difficulties talking about their feelings. Children and adolescents diagnosed with AS may internalize the chaos that is going on around them during the divorce and may blame themselves for the breakup of the parents' or caregivers' marriage.

A fourteen-year-old young man diagnosed with AS was referred to me as a result of his parents' divorce. He was an only child, and his parents were concerned because he would not talk about the situation and had appeared indifferent to the news that they were splitting up. They wanted to know his thoughts about primary residence and were willing to allow the young man to choose which parent he wanted live with the majority of the time, or if he wanted to split time with each parent, living with his mother for one week and with his father for another week. The young man and I began working together and it soon became apparent that he was experiencing grief but was confused by this emotion. He revealed to me that he had never experienced grief before, neither from the death of a friend or family member, and he had never experienced the loss or death of a pet, he had not even lost a favorite toy. I realized that he was experiencing the emotion, but the emotion completely baffled him. Thus, he appeared non-caring and aloof, paralyzed by not being able to process the thoughts and feelings and definitely unable to even begin answering the questions that his parents were asking him. This is an example of how a divorce-triggered grief that left this young man confused and unable to move forward.

Fear is another devastating emotion that the divorce experience can trigger in children and teens. For the child or adolescent diagnosed with AS, the fear that is experienced is often related to a lack of understanding of unconditional love and the change in routine or familiar places due to having to split time between parents. Children and adolescents diagnosed with AS often view people and relationships as "things;" and because of mindblindness and alexithymia, they have difficulty understanding the intricacies of relationships. Mom and dad are just "there" and many assume they always will be, like the big tree out front or the red brick building on the corner of the street where they live. The child or adolescent diagnosed with AS can sometimes be terrified by the idea of divorce because to them, relationships are already scary because they do not understand them. Therefore, many adopt the thinking "If mom and dad can pick up and leave each other, then how can I be sure that they won't leave me?" Therapists who work with divorce will recognize this same line of thinking in young children, who are often too young to understand the different types of love, the varying degrees of love between a man and a woman, and the love between a parent and a child.

Divorce usually disrupts the routines of children and adolescents. Even the most dedicated parents find that some disruption of their children and adolescents' lives is inevitable. Changes in meal times, pick-up times, and free time represent just a few of the adjustments to routines that children and adolescents must make. Resilient children and adolescents of divorce can bend with the changes and make the necessary adjustments. Typically, children and adolescents diagnosed with AS are the least able to make these adjustments. For these children and adolescents the fight-or-flight response triggers over and over, creating emotional, cognitive, and physiological upheaval resulting in acting out behaviors. Children and adolescents diagnosed with AS often exhibit regressed behavior during this time of upheaval, becoming toddler-like in behavior such as engaging in non-verbal communication, wetting the bed, and refusing to perform tasks such as bathing or dressing themselves.

Behavioral Effects

Emotional upheaval is evidenced through behavior. The behavior of children and adolescents diagnosed with AS who are dealing with divorce can be seen in the same areas as neurotypical children and adolescents: School difficulties, temper tantrums, social withdrawal, and expressive difficulties are just a few of the behavioral problems that children and adolescents diagnosed with AS exhibit when they are experiencing divorce. Parents of children and adolescents diagnosed with AS face special challenges dealing with behavioral problems as a result of divorce. Due to difficulties previously discussed, children and adolescents diagnosed with AS often have a lack of insight into their behavior and emotions, and have deficits in expressive abilities. This often leaves parents feeling incapable of understanding these behaviors as well as feeling frustrated and helpless due to being unable to get the behaviors to stop. "If he could just tell me *why* he does what he does maybe I could understand it and help him to stop doing this!" a distraught mother said to me recently. Some parents of children or adolescents diagnosed with AS are concerned because there is no emotional or behavioral reaction at all. I remind them that this does not necessarily mean that there is anything wrong, but it is worth exploring just to make sure. It must be remembered that children and adolescents diagnosed with AS often struggle with communicating thoughts and feelings just like their neurotypical peers, especially when an experience like divorce occurs.

A common behavior that I have witnessed in children and adolescents diagnosed with AS experiencing divorce is withdrawal and isolation from family, friends, and activities. This is usually related to a mixture of anxiety and depression being experienced by the child or adolescent. Because of the difficulties in understanding emotions, the child or adolescent shuts down and avoids contact with people, even people with whom they are familiar. Children and adolescents diagnosed with AS may also withdraw from activities that they previously enjoyed, a significant symptom of depressed thinking. I worked with one young man diagnosed with AS whose parents suddenly separated and his mother was very concerned because he had stopped playing the computer game that had been, in her words, "his whole life" for four years. He shared with me that he suddenly found no fulfillment in the game and this bothered him and intrigued him at the same time. It was the first time in his life that he felt "sadness" which he defined as having no joy or fulfillment in living. Prior to the separation of his parents, he read and heard about people being "sad" but only could imagine what it was like.

The intensity of stereotyped interests and OCD tendencies may increase for children and adolescents diagnosed with AS when experiencing the effects of divorce. As routines are forced to change for many children and adolescents because of the divorce, the child or adolescent clings to anything that can make them feel safe. Thus, the need to play their favorite video game becomes more intense, the need to count "extra" steps before putting their pants on becomes imperative for survival, and so on. I worked with one young man whose parents had separated and were planning on divorcing and he developed five new OCD behaviors in one week, and the behaviors that were already present increased in intensity. While this is to be expected due to the emotional upheaval that often accompanies divorce, it is also a sign of intense emotional turmoil within the child or adolescent diagnosed with AS.

Relational Effects

Relationships are built on trust. Divorce causes a child or adolescent to reevaluate not only whom they trust but to think about trust in a new way. An adolescent diagnosed with AS shared with me that when his parents divorced, he felt he could still trust them in that he knew they were not going to harm or kill him, but he did not know if he could trust that they would follow through on plans or promises about matters in the future. For instance, he said that prior to the divorce if his father said they were going to Dairy Queen on Saturday, the young man never questioned it and fully believed that his father would take him there. Following the divorce, he chose not to believe these types of promises or plans. Until he saw the Dairy Queen sign and his father's car entered the parking lot, only then did he believe that his father was actually taking him there. This type of thinking generalized to other situations such as church and school, and with people whom the young man had relationships with, such as teachers or his youth group leader.

While neurotypical children and adolescents tend to struggle with trust following the divorce experience, it is more profound for the child or adolescent diagnosed with AS because of complications caused by mindblindness and alexithymia that disrupt the building and sustaining of relationships. The relationship with the parents or caregivers tends to be the most significant relationship for the child or adolescent diagnosed with AS, and divorce threatens this bond. Some children diagnosed with AS develop severe separation anxiety when faced with being away from one of the parents or caregivers because of the visitation schedules that accompany separation or divorce of parents. A seven-year-old child diagnosed with AS was referred to me due to emotional difficulties because of his parents' divorce. He was experiencing separation anxiety when he had to be away from his mother. This began during the first visitation weekend with his father following their separation, and subsequently the child was afraid to be left anywhere without his mother, even school. The parents were shocked because they explained to the boy in detail how the separation was going to work and that he would be staying with his father on most weekends and with mother during the week. Both parents said the boy acknowledged that he understood them and went back to playing with his toys. However, when it came time for his mother to leave after dropping him off at his father's apartment, the boy became hysterical. Following this incident, he refused to go to school because of the fear of being away from his mother, despite the fact that he had gone to school for almost two years and never had any problems when it was time for his mother to leave.

PARENT AND CAREGIVER CONSIDERATIONS

I have found that parents and caregivers benefit from reassurance and guidance from the therapist working with their child or adolescent diagnosed with AS when they experience divorce. A parent or caregiver going through a divorce is often experiencing emotional upheaval as well as the child or adolescent, and the coping skills of that parent or caregiver are tested during this chaotic time. For the parent or caregiver of the child or adolescent diagnosed with AS, there are extra challenges that AS brings, and many parents and caregivers report feeling an extra weight because they believe they may cause irreparable damage to their child or adolescent. I often remind parents and caregivers who are going through a divorce that it is normal for their child or adolescent (whether diagnosed with AS or neurotypical) to display some emotional and behavioral difficulties. I remind the parent or caregiver that this means their child is normal! Parents and caregivers also need to be aware of the emotional and behavioral effects of divorce and how the challenges of AS create special challenges for the child or adolescent. I coach parents and caregivers about depression, anxiety, and the risk of suicide for their child or adolescent diagnosed with AS, and I emphasize connection and communication by the parent or caregiver to the child or adolescent during the divorce experience. If schedules and routines are going to change significantly, I encourage parents and caregivers to walk the child or adolescent through those new routines and changes ahead of time, so that there is ample time for preparation.

THERAPIST CONSIDERATIONS

Therapists who work with children and adolescents diagnosed with AS going through the divorce experience should be aware of several things. One important consideration is that the experience of divorce can cause intense emotional, behavioral, and social reactions in children and adolescents diagnosed with AS. Children and adolescents diagnosed with AS are not robots and can be deeply affected by the loss that divorce brings. Many people judge the effect of an experience upon a person's reaction to that experience, and just because some children and adolescents diagnosed with AS show little or no reaction, one should not assume that the child or adolescent is not affected. Of course the opposite reaction of assuming that a child or adolescent should be having significant problems because of the divorce is also problematic. The therapist should assess each child or adolescent diagnosed with AS on an individual basis and be careful to not make assumptions.

A second consideration for therapists working with children and adolescents diagnosed with AS going through the divorce process is to remember to be patient in getting the child or adolescent to share their thoughts and feelings. I will discuss this more in the section of the play therapy techniques. The therapist must not push the child or adolescent diagnosed with AS to reveal too much too soon as the emotions can be overwhelming at times. The therapist's patience also allows for trust building to occur between the child or adolescent and the therapist. Building a solid therapeutic alliance of trust and safety is of utmost importance when working with children and adolescents diagnosed with AS who are experiencing the rough waters of divorce, and the patience of the therapist is very important in allowing this to happen. At times our efforts as therapists have very good intentions because we want so desperately to help the young person who is hurting and we try to do too much in too little time, causing setbacks in the therapeutic process. This is why play therapy is so wonderful, because the child or adolescent is at the helm. I am there, but they are steering, listening, watching, and speaking when they are ready; and I am invited into this sacred place of healing.

A final consideration for therapists who are working with a child or adolescent diagnosed with AS going through the divorce process is to remember the important role that empathy plays in connecting with these amazing young people at such a critical time in their lives. Empathy is not only a key ingredient in building the therapeutic relationship but is an important quality for the therapist to model for the child or adolescent when dealing with intense emotional content such as divorce or grief/loss. The relationship with the therapist is a powerful picture of both building and maintaining a relationship.

Modeling relation-building attributes and qualities gives the child or adolescent a reference point of what a quality like empathy looks like and, hopefully, allows them to know what it feels like to receive it.

PLAY THERAPY TO HELP CHILDREN WITH DIVORCE ISSUES

Play to Help with Emotional Effects

Children represent a population that is at risk when a divorce occurs because of having fewer coping skills due to a lack of mental and emotional maturity. Divorce can also disrupt development by causing setbacks or stagnation during several important developmental milestones. Safety and trust are often derived from the relationship of the child's parents or caregivers and these two elements are key ingredients to the child's ability to learn, connect, and grow. Children diagnosed with AS are a special population that can benefit greatly from an empathic therapist who provides a sanctuary of safety and connection when experiencing the rough waters that divorce can bring. As previously discussed, emotions experienced during this time can bring confusion and terror that can result in behavioral acting out or shutting down. The following play therapy techniques are designed to help the therapist deal specifically with many of the issues that divorce can bring and help the child diagnosed with AS weather the storm and provide coping skills, emotional understanding, and a sense of safety.

Sand Play

I discussed in Chapter Four how I use sand play with children diagnosed with AS and how new research is emerging regarding the effectiveness of sand play with children diagnosed with AS (Lu, et al. 2009). Sand play is effective for children who are experiencing chaotic events in their lives such as divorce because it allows them to create a world that is theirs alone and the child has the freedom to add to or take away from that world objects that represent pieces of their own fragmented world. Children can also destroy the world they have created (Norton and Norton, 1997). It is impossible to predict if a child diagnosed with AS is going to engage in sand play; in fact, I have found that some cannot tolerate the feeling of sand on their hands. Some of these children will use a tool such as a stick or scooping spoon to manipulate the sand. I have encountered some children diagnosed with AS that simply take one look at the sandbox and walk away. I may begin playing in the sand to see if the child will join me, but if they do not engage after a few minutes, I do not force them.

It has long been believed that sand play is not effective for children diagnosed with AS, but I always introduce it and evaluate its effectiveness on a case-by-case basis. I feel that for issues like divorce as well as grief and loss, sand play can be a powerful healing medium for children diagnosed with AS and is worth introducing to the child as it can be a very effective tool to use with the child. We as therapists must remember that each child is different and we need our clinical training, but we also need to be imaginative and creative with these unique and amazing young people. The use of sand play may be the medium that means the most to the child—it may be that sand play provides the child diagnosed with AS dealing with the experience of divorce, with just the right ingredients to learn to understand the emotions they are feeling and to cope with the change and loss that divorce can bring.

Sand Play and Divorce: A Case Study

A seven-year-old child diagnosed with AS was struggling with his parents' divorce. Like many divorces, it dragged on for almost two years. When his parents initially separated he had great difficulty resulting in academic, emotional, and behavioral difficulties. His parents reported that they did nothing, and eventually "he went back to normal." It appeared that he had grown accustomed to the separation but when he discovered that the "actual divorce" was going through in a few weeks through overhearing his mother and father arguing during a phone call, all of the initial symptoms that he displayed when the parents first separated returned. Both parents decided to place him in counseling for help with his academic, emotional, and behavioral difficulties. Like many divorcing parents, the frequency of arguments on the phone between them and hateful comments made in the presence of the young boy had increased as the date of the actual divorce grew closer. I introduced him to the sand box and he was initially interested because of the Army jeeps, tanks, and soldiers that were in a container next to the box. He told me "I really like war stuff" and began organizing the toys into rows next to the sandbox. I stayed quiet and watched him, secretly wondering if he would include the sandbox in his play.

After lining everything up, he then reproduced the same rows in the sandbox, gently placing the items in the sand exactly the same distance apart. He then turned them, keeping them the same distance apart. I noticed that his hands never touched the sand, only the pieces when he placed them in the sand. He then lifted each piece to examine the grains of sand sticking to the bottom of them and then put them back in the same place. Using behavioral tracking, I would remark "You are picking them up" and "You are making sure they are the same distance apart." This went on until the end of the session when it was time for him to go home. I was intrigued because he did not actually play with the army toys, only lined them up and turned them, picked them up and put them back where they were. During the next session, he began with the same behavior but this time laid the soldiers down being careful to not let his hands touch the sand. He held the soldier flat and allowed it to fall face up and then took his index finger and poked it down into the sand. All of the soldiers were exactly the same distance apart. I used behavioral tracking for each of these sequences. He then took a small shovel and scooped up some sand and began to sprinkle it over all of the soldiers, eventually covering them completely. I wondered aloud "I wonder why they are all covered up?" and the boy responded "They are dead." When he finally finished, it was time for him to go home.

During the third session, the boy was eager to get to the sand box and the army toys. Instead of lining up or gently placing the soldiers in the sand, he lifted the whole container and dumped all the toys in the middle of the sandbox. He then took the same shovel and began to pour the sand over the toys in an attempt to bury them. Again he buried everything but was not as organized as in the previous sessions. He said the "war had happened and everything was destroyed." "What is going to happen next I wonder" I said inquisitively, "Oh, you know, gotta pick up the dead guys, stuff like that" he said matter-of-factly. It was during this third session when he dumped all the toys in a chaotic manner that he began to touch the sand, and the carefulness that he had demonstrated had disappeared. He bulldozed the army toys, buried them, dug them up, and bulldozed them again. He threw the soldiers up in the air when they "blew up." I had introduced water to the sand play which intrigued him. He liked having a bucket of water nearby to dip his hands in when they go "too sandy" which I could tell by him staring at the grains of sand on his hands and him constantly rubbing them on his pants. I watched him closely to assess for overstimulation, but he always re-engaged in the play after pausing to wipe his hands.

He began to act out detailed battle sequences and took a great deal of time setting up the battle field, complete with trenches, hiding places, and secret stocks of ammunition. During the fifth session after creating a pre-battlefield masterpiece, he just stared at it with the most contented and peaceful look in his eyes and remarked "I gotta get a sandbox at home." He never invited me into the play, only telling me to get this toy or that one, or to hand him the shovel. By the fifth session he said to me "You just sit there and watch me, okay?" and I agreed that I would just sit and watch, but I continue to use behavioral tracking which he did not mind. I have worked with some children diagnosed with AS who show great annoyance at behavioral tracking and actually tell me not to do it, and I honor their request! Over the next six sessions this young boy continued his war play but it became more and more orderly and eventually evolved into him just making the battlefield and never getting around to the war. He also switched from the war theme to building with Lincoln Logs in the sandbox and making sand towers which he would carve with a plastic knife and other tools.

Throughout these sessions I connected with his parents frequently to find out how he was doing at home and school. The parents were worried initially because his emotional outbursts and behavior worsened after he entered therapy. I warn parents that this can happen, and I prepare them with parenting skills and tools to handle more intense emotional and behavioral outbursts in case it does happen. When a child's emotional and behavioral acting out increases after entering therapy, I welcome it and view it in a positive light because the layers of resistance are being removed and the real issues are being touched and confronted by the child. The parents shared that following the fourth or fifth session something amazing had happened; the boy's emotional and behavioral outbursts had lessened in intensity and frequency, and the school reported the same information. By the twelfth session, the parents reported that it had been a full two weeks without any emotional or behavioral problems and that their son appeared contented and while an occasional emotional or behavioral outburst still happened, it was shorter in duration and much less intense than before.

Sand play enabled this boy to release the feelings that came from the chaotic environment in which he was living. Later sessions revealed that he had internalized his parents' arguing and fighting, believing that he was the reason for their not being able to get along. He had long ago accepted the divorce. However, the verbal fighting on the phone, negative comments both parents made to others and to him, and evidence of negative emotions that both parents wore on their faces contributed to his inner turmoil. The sandbox provided a place for him to find control as evidenced in the early behavior of carefully placing the soldiers and toys in perfect order; it provided a place to express grief and loss as evidenced by the burying behavior of the "dead" soldiers; and it provided a place to release the internalized feelings of anger and guilt as evidenced by the wars that he played out over and over again. Through playing in the sand box, the boy also demonstrated his feelings of peace, contentment, and acceptance as evidenced by the shift in his sand play from war to creating houses, buildings, and sculptures in the sand.

This case represents how non-directive sand play was utilized with a boy diagnosed with AS struggling with his parents' divorce. I mentioned earlier that modifications may have to be made with children diagnosed with AS due to their inability to engage in spontaneous play, but this boy took to the sand play immediately and not once did I guide him or lead him to it. Not once did I mention divorce, the arguing of his parents, or tried to get him to talk about his feelings of either. I only sat with him, watching and being fully present, verbally tracking his behavior which provided reassurance and proved to him that I really was present and sent the message that he was safe. I was an awe-struck witness to this sacred process of healing that sand play provided, and I felt an overwhelming sensation of gratefulness and awe, much like Bradway and McCoard (1997) describe.

Play to Help with Behavioral Effects

I discussed earlier in the chapter how many children diagnosed with AS exhibit behavioral problems during the divorce experience. A divorce forces change and children diagnosed with AS characteristically do not cope well with unexpected changes. Tantrums, withdrawal, regressing to earlier developmental stages, and physical aggression may be exhibited by the child diagnosed with AS who is experiencing the effects of divorce. Of course, therapists see the emotional turmoil that drives the outward behavior, but parents, caregivers, and educators do not always understand this. I help parents and caregivers understand that the behavior that the child is exhibiting is directly related to the triggering of the sympathetic nervous system and the child's brain going into the fight-or-flight mode. Thus, this survival response becomes aroused because of a disrupted routine (a situation that the child cannot control) which triggers fear ("I am not safe") and the child demonstrates the acting out behaviors. The techniques that follow are designed to help the child gain better coping skills in understanding the difference between *feeling* unsafe and the reality of being unsafe. These techniques actually combine both behavioral and emotional work, but I have included them here in the behavioral section because behaviors are a common reason for a referral to therapy when a child is experiencing the effects of a divorce.

Video Games

I discussed in Chapter Five the use of video games such as Lego Star Wars and Lego Indiana Jones to help the child diagnosed with AS conquer fear. Lego Star Wars has the element of using the "force" to conquer enemies, and Lego Indiana Jones uses the element of Indiana Jones' intellect and ingenuity to get through seemingly impossible situations. Games such as these put the child in a position to utilize good decision making and instead of reacting fearfully to the various enemies and obstacles that are put in the way to thwart success, the child achieves success through making controlled, rational decisions. The goal is to help the child diagnosed with AS generalize this to a real-world application by helping them see that despite how fearful a change in routine or schedule can be, the reality is that they are not in danger.

I used video games with a child diagnosed with AS whose parents were divorcing which created upheaval in his ordered world due to a change in routine and living arrangements. He responded with tantrums and aggressive behavior at home and school. He liked video games and especially liked Lego Indiana Jones. We played together using the two-player option, and each time a danger popped up, I paused the game and pointed this out to him. We then worked together to get past the obstacle or danger and I paused the game again to talk about what we did to get past the obstacle. I then asked him about obstacles in his life because of his parents' divorce and he shared things such as having to live in a new house and not being able to do the same things every day. I pointed out to him that those obstacles are a lot like Indiana Jones getting through the snake pit because he did not realize there were going to be snakes down there. "But Indy never panics," I said. We talked about panic and fear and how he *feels* afraid when something is new or different but he does not change, only the situation changes. Indiana Jones never changes, but the situations and obstacles do, and he always is able to overcome them. This helped the young man begin to gain insight in understanding his fears and learning that he can choose other behaviors when he feels afraid instead of lashing out.

Earthquake!

Two themes that cause coping difficulties for children diagnosed with AS who are experiencing divorce are unexpected change/transition and the need to create a "new normal." For anyone who has experienced a divorce, building a "new normal" in the aftermath of the destruction can be a lot like sifting through the ruins following a natural disaster and starting over. Life will never be the same, but at some point the individual must attempt to begin putting things back together. Over time, a "new normal" emerges in which the individual has accepted the loss and starts over. This activity helps to model this idea for the child diagnosed with AS and helps them play out in a fun way the terrifying themes of unexpected change and building a "new normal."

I begin with building blocks and a piece of thin particle board or cardboard. I instruct the child to build a structure on the board using the blocks, and I build one also. Once the structure is built, I take my piece of board and begin to move it, showing the child how it sways with the movement. I move it a little harder and show how some of the blocks begin to fall, and the blocks at the bottom begin to shift in position. I encourage the child to do the same, experimenting with how fragile building blocks are without cement or glue to hold them in place. I tell them that this is just how we are as human beings and we like things that are stable and routine and something like divorce is like an *earthquake* that threatens to knock us over and makes us afraid. This opens the door for the child to communicate about their divorce experience and how it has affected them.

The next phase of the activity is "rebuilding." This involves taking the fallen blocks (many children enjoy completely demolishing their structure and make the blocks go flying) and building the structure again to make it earthquake-safe. Sometimes a child may build the structure in a more solid manner by stacking heavier blocks on the bottom, or not building the structure as high. I use this phase of the activity to demonstrate how we have to "start over" after something like divorce and even though some things are different, many things stay the same. I take a block and set it down and say "Mom and Dad still love you even though they are not going to live together." Then I take another block and say "School is exactly the same, it is not going anywhere." And then with another block I say "You still get to have your video games (or whatever the stereotyped interest is) but it is just at different times than when you were used to." This is to help represent the solid blocks in the child's life that are really there and to build a foundation of reassurance and safety for the child so they can begin to create a "new normal" out of the ruins. One boy that I worked with suddenly jumped up, ran to my desk and grabbed the Scotch tape dispenser and ran back and began to tape his blocks together. This provided a picture of adapting to change and I was able to use the tape as a metaphor for positive thoughts, feelings, behaviors, and people that help us through difficult trials in life.

Play to Help with Relational Effects

Divorce affects all who are involved and the emotional and mental strain tends to create isolation effects among family members. Each person, mother and father, son or daughter is hurting in their own way and is struggling to cope with the changes that divorce can bring. The child diagnosed with AS can often get shoved aside in the storm of divorce because of difficulties in communicating wants and needs and by parents and caregivers assuming that the child is "okay" because of this lack of communication. I have found that parents and caregivers are often at a loss during times of extreme stress like divorce to know how to connect with a child or adolescent diagnosed with AS and meeting their emotional needs. I have found that including family members in the therapy process can be very helpful for the child diagnosed with AS to provide a sense of stability despite the unexpected changes that divorce can bring.

Play That Builds Connection

I wrote in Chapter Five about the *Play That Builds Connection* technique that helps to connect parents and caregivers to the child diagnosed with AS. This technique is useful when the family is going through the divorce experience because it can give parents and caregivers the opportunity to put their feelings into words and reinforce safety and connection with the child through the play experience. Many parents and caregivers of children diagnosed with AS struggle with knowing how to connect through play and this process not only gives the parent and caregiver valuable tools in this area but also creates resiliency against stress in the relationship and the individual parent or caregiver through joining in the miracle of play. The deeper connections that are built between the child and the parent or caregiver through play provide a great sense of safety for the child and reinforce trust in the parent or caregiver. I share the view of Ahrons (2007; Ahrons and Marquardt, 2010) that divorce, while being a disruptive force in a child's life, provides an opportunity for the child to gain emotional strength and that therapy can be directed towards creating a positive, strength-based approach.

Play that Builds Connection with parents and caregivers of children diagnosed with AS experiencing divorce involves that parent or caregiver being connected in the therapeutic play experience with the child and being taught techniques that can be utilized in the home environment. I have witnessed the power of play being able to cushion the blow of divorce for children diagnosed with AS through parents and caregivers incorporating this miraculous tool into their daily routine with the child. Sometimes the issues between parents are too complicated and the emotional climate too charged and intense to have them both in the playroom with the child at the same time, particularly in the early stages of separation or divorce. I meet with each parent separately when this is the case to not make things worse for the child. Playing board games and video games together, as well as getting the parent to join the child in spontaneous and repetitive play in the form of sand play and building with Lego bricks, Tinker Toys, or Lincoln Logs are all part of this amazing healing, strengthening process.

Group Play

I have discussed group play in previous chapters and will discuss it briefly here as well as later in the chapter when I discuss grief and loss issues. Group play provides the child diagnosed with AS all of the benefits previously mentioned, but in addition it includes the element of identifying with other children who are going through divorce and produces an opportunity for gaining valuable coping skills that lead toward developing resiliency. I am always fascinated by the surprised and relieved look on the faces of children diagnosed with AS when they hear another child talking about the same problem they are experiencing, whether it is divorce, grief or loss, or a bullying problem. I find it a wonderful opportunity to have the child see empathy and sympathy modeled by the therapist and to be taught appropriate social responses when being in the presence of another who is experiencing emotional pain.

PLAY THERAPY TO HELP ADOLESCENTS WITH DIVORCE ISSUES

Play to Help with Emotional Effects

I discussed in previous chapters some of the emotional struggles that plague adolescents diagnosed with AS. Emotional regulation deficits and emotional immaturity disrupt the adolescent's ability to form and sustain relationships, potentially creating a great deal of confusion and a sense of failure as the adolescent enters a time of life with increasingly complex social situations and demands. The experience of divorce can be devastating for any young person, but for the adolescent diagnosed with AS the emotional effects caused by the divorce experience can be particularly difficult. The lack of understanding of their own emotions and the emotions of others, as well as being easily overwhelmed by emotions make the experience of divorce a confusing and frightening thing for the adolescent diagnosed with AS. The following techniques are designed to help the therapist assist the adolescent in weathering the emotional storms that divorce can bring by helping them understand emotions and learn coping skills in dealing with unpleasant emotions.

Computer and Video Games

The Sims Game

I discussed in Chapter Seven how I have used The Sims game with adolescents struggling with emotional issues. I have found The Sims particularly useful with adolescents diagnosed with AS dealing with divorce for a number of reasons. First, as previously mentioned, the game gives the young person a chance to create a representation of themselves as well as a "world" that the young person can experiment with and manipulate which can provide a sense of control. A second characteristic of The Sims game making it useful for work with teens diagnosed with AS dealing with divorce is that it is possible to have the adolescent re-create the family dynamics and the situations surrounding the divorce. Individuals diagnosed with AS sometimes struggle with communicating thoughts and feelings and many become frustrated talking about the situation because of the confusing emotions that can surface. The game provides a wonderful way to "show" the therapist and allow the game to speak for the adolescent.

A third characteristic making The Sims useful is the opportunity for the therapist to get the adolescent to talk about the emotions that accompany the experience of divorce. As I mentioned earlier, it is important to not assume that an adolescent dealing with divorce is having a hard time emotionally. Sometimes I wonder if the adolescent diagnosed with AS weathers circumstances like divorce better because of the attributes of AS. The Sims game allows the adolescent to paint the picture of what the divorce experience is like for them and makes it a personal account through the medium of game play. For instance, a fourteen-year-old diagnosed with AS was able to show me the dynamics of going between her father's house and her mother's house and her feeling frustrated about the differences in rules and expectations at both houses. She demonstrated a great deal of emotional immaturity and I wonder if she would have been able to connect as deeply with her frustration about the matter without The Sims game to provide the opportunity to do so. I discuss The Sims game as a play-therapy tool for addressing emotional content later in the chapter when I address grief and loss issues.

Sand Play

I have previously discussed the usefulness of sand play with children diagnosed with AS experiencing the effects of divorce and demonstrated its usefulness in helping process emotional content. Sand play is most often associated with children; however,; there is a good deal of research that shows sand play is useful with adolescents as well as adults (Bradway and McCoard, 1997). I have found sand play useful with adolescents diagnosed with AS who are experiencing emotional upheaval as a result of divorce. Sand play provides the adolescent with a way to create a world of their own, complete with various themes and objects that have meaning to the adolescent and represent the inner emotional conflicts with which they are dealing. While some adolescents diagnosed with AS require some direction to get started in sand play, I often find that they become just as involved and interested in the sand play as children.

One fourteen-year-old young man diagnosed with AS was referred for issues related to his parents' divorce. He was evidencing depressed-mood symptoms through a lack of interest in things he used to enjoy as well as withdrawal from family and friends. He was extremely shut down upon meeting me and said very little; I had offered to play games with him such as chess or cards and he declined. He became interested in the sandbox upon finding a Lego vehicle sitting in the sand box. He eventually moved toward the sand box after being curious, and I encouraged him to investigate the vehicle. He began to make a road and then a bridge using Lincoln Logs. He spent a great deal of time on the bridge and made sure that it was reinforced before moving the Lego vehicle over the bridge. He said nothing as he did this, and I sat quietly on the floor with him just watching. He then added a few structures using the Lincoln Logs and made a road that connected all of the structures. He spent a great deal of time on the road, smoothing it over and over and carefully driving the Lego vehicle over it. For the next few sessions he made roads and structures and gradually began to talk more and more about the intense emotions that he was experiencing. The sand play loosened him up and allowed him to feel free to gradually speak about the emotions he was experiencing. He later told me that the sand comforted him and making the roads and structures reminded him of when he would play as a small boy and how he felt so contented back then. He actually thanked me for having the freedom to play in the sand and said that being reminded of what it felt like when he was young gave him a peace about the future that things would be okay, and he expressed confidence that he would get through this difficult time.

Play to Help with Behavioral Effects

Adolescents, just as children, can display many different types of behavior when experiencing divorce. Physical displays may include hitting, pushing, punching things, slamming doors, refusing to engage in schoolwork, or withdrawal from family or friends and avoiding activities that the adolescent used to enjoy. I discussed in the section about children with behavioral issues that the therapist recognizes these behaviors as the outward manifestation of the inward churning of emotions, but often parents refer the adolescent because of behavior problems and only focus on those. Adolescents diagnosed with AS can display the above behaviors much like their neurotypical peers, but the behaviors displayed by the adolescent diagnosed with AS can sometimes be more frustrating for parents and caregivers because of the difficulties adolescents diagnosed with AS often have with understanding emotions and communicating thoughts and feelings to their parent or caregiver. The following techniques are designed to help the adolescent diagnosed with AS learn coping skills that lead them toward making better behavioral choices and helping them learn to self-soothe and be non-reactive when experiencing negative emotions.

Video Games

Tetris

I discussed in Chapter Seven how Tetris can be useful in helping an adolescent diagnosed with AS gain skills in regulating their emotions. I have found this very useful with adolescents dealing with divorce and who are making poor behavioral choices because of overwhelming emotions. As previously described, the adolescent is purposely frustrated and the therapist is able to introduce the concept of the fight-or-flight response and teach the adolescent how to self-soothe while practicing concentrating on the game. The game also has the theme of working on choice making through how the player fits the pieces together in order to clear lines. Some pieces need to be flipped and shifted in order to make the best fit and the player must be able to ascertain which pattern calls for which piece and how that piece will be fit into the puzzle. This helps introduce the concept of choosing positive behavior choices despite feeling negative emotions. Because of the game, this is done in a fun, non-threatening manner, and the therapist is available to guide the adolescent and encourage them in this process.

I used Tetris with an adolescent diagnosed with AS struggling with his parents' divorce who was exhibiting aggressive behavior with younger siblings and peers at school. He would shove or hit others and had also begun digging his nails into his arms and legs when becoming frustrated. It was not hard to get him to recognize that this was not healthy behavior, and, in fact, he showed a great deal of remorse *after* his poor behavior choices. This is common in children and adolescents who are diagnosed with AS, in addition to neurotypical children and adolescents, who act out behaviorally because of poor emotional regulation. Once the child or adolescent is out of fight-or-flight mode, the parasympathetic nervous system reengages and they are able to see the results of their poor choices. For the adolescent diagnosed with AS, and this was true for this young man, there is often extreme negative self-attribution and self-loathing because of the presence of all-or-nothing thinking ("I am either all good or all bad") after the behavior is exhibited, which instead of leading to insight and better emotional regulation, only leads to a lower self-worth and emotional confusion.

I was able to set up the frustration sequence as I described in Chapter Seven, and he quickly became frustrated and wanted to quit the game. It is important when using techniques such as this with the adolescent diagnosed with AS that the therapist be mindful to not over stimulate the young person. I was able to connect him to these feelings of frustration and help him see that this is what was happening just prior to him loosing emotional control and lashing out at his younger siblings and peers at school. We began at the easiest levels of the game and gradually worked up to the harder levels where the pieces fell faster. At each level, he was able to gradually feel his frustration but was able to calm himself. When he made a mistake, he no longer threw down the controller in frustration but was able to stay calm and work through the mistake and stay in control. He began to connect the *feeling* of being in control as well as *doing* the mental work of keeping himself calm and not reacting. His behavioral outbursts quickly stopped at school following three sessions of using this technique. The lashing out at siblings became less frequent and his mother reported recognizing him becoming angry but choosing other behaviors instead of hurting himself or others. He, like all adolescents, continued to struggle at times regulating emotions and choosing appropriate behaviors, but he improved in this area very much. Through this process of using Tetris, a valuable foundation was laid for this young man to begin to understand his frustration, learn to self-soothe, and to learn to choose appropriate behaviors.

Games with Choice Components

Adolescents diagnosed with AS that make poor behavioral choices can benefit from playing games that contain choice components. Any game that forces a player to make choices and feel the consequences of those choices are useful to help the adolescent make the connection between the game and real life. Board games, card games, and computer and video games are useful for this process. I demonstrated the use of chess in previous chapters as a useful tool because of the themes of choice, being rewarded for careful planning, practicing anticipating another's moves, and seeing a situation from a different perspective. I also like to use simple games such as checkers, Chinese checkers, or tic-tac-toe as these are quick and easy to teach if the adolescent is not familiar with the game. Simple games also contain the themes that are necessary to build a good foundation of understanding the connection between choices and consequences. The goal is the adolescent will learn the concepts from the games and generalize those to real life situations, learning to make better choices and avoiding negative consequences that come from poor choices.

Play to Help with Relational Effects

Play that Builds Connection (Adolescent Version)

A divorce represents a potential disruption of many different relationships and a time of readjusting for all involved. For the adolescent diagnosed with AS, the divorce experience potentially disrupts an already fragile relationship ecosystem between themselves and the parent or caregiver. I have found that most parents and caregivers I encounter who are experiencing divorce do want to connect with the adolescent diagnosed with AS on a deeper level, but they do not know how. The emotional turmoil that the parent or caregiver is experiencing can create a block in their ability to connect. Also the adolescent diagnosed with AS is sometimes in shutdown mode because of the emotions that surface due to disruptions in relations and routines. The therapy office represents a wonderful place for the parent or caregiver and the teen diagnosed with AS to come together and build a deeper connection through play.

The *Play That Builds Connection* technique with adolescents is very much the same as the technique I described earlier in previous chapters. The parent becomes part of the play process, and the adolescent and parent or caregiver engage in play and activities that are designed to facilitate communication as well as build a closer bond. I use board games, computer and video games, card games, as well as art projects such as painting, clay sculpting, or drawing pictures together. This technique helps to send the message to the adolescent that the parent is present, and despite the disruption in living arrangements and routines, it helps to reassure the adolescent that the relationship with the parent or caregiver is intact. It also helps to build trust and forms a foundation on which other relationships can be built. This type of play puts the adult in the adolescent's world and creates a level-playing field, devoid of power and control; instead focusing on the interaction of the two individuals.

I used video games with a father and his adolescent son diagnosed with AS. Because of the recent divorce, the father and son were forced to spend time together on the weekends, which was a new experience for both of them. Their relationship became strained over the past few years, partly due to the father's work schedule and partly due to the young man being more interested in computer and video games than connecting with his father. The father admitted not knowing how to connect with his son. The young man's mother had suggested joint therapy sessions to help build a closer relationship between them, and the father agreed. I used the video game that the young man enjoyed and set up the sessions with the father and son playing the game together. This put the adolescent in the teaching role, and the father in the student role. The sessions consisted of the father and son playing the game together and I helped facilitate communication through modeling and prompting questions from them. Over a series of sessions, the communication level between the two increased, and the relationship improved greatly. I prescribed specific play times for them during the weekend visits, which gradually generalized to other activities such as going to movies, car shows, and nature walks. This activity worked well to enhance the relationship between the father and son, and the young man remarked that he never knew how smart his dad really was until he spent more time with him. The young man's father stated that he was overjoyed to be able to connect with his son in a new way and felt empowered that he could be a force in his son's life. He admitted that the barriers of AS had made him feel like he had nothing in common with his son and that he had nothing to offer him because the father was not interested in video games; another relationship enhanced through the power of play!

Group Play

Group play is a wonderful technique to use with adolescents who are experiencing struggles such as divorce, and grief/loss. I will discuss later in the chapter the power of group play with adolescents diagnosed with AS who are experiencing grief or loss issues. I have found that the group play experience for adolescents diagnosed with AS provides empowerment through being able to connect and share with others who are experiencing many of the same difficulties. For adolescents diagnosed with AS experiencing divorce, group play can be helpful putting feelings into words through hearing others share similar feelings and perspectives of the divorce experience. Group play also serves as a way for adolescents diagnosed with AS to form friendships that can expand outside of the group and serve as a meeting place for these amazing young people.

GRIEF AND LOSS AND CHILDREN AND ADOLESCENTS DIAGNOSED WITH ASPERGER'S SYNDROME

Children and adolescents diagnosed with AS do feel sadness when experiencing loss, and children and adolescents diagnosed with AS do grieve. I recently encountered a young man diagnosed with AS who was very upset over the fact that a show that had become dear to him was about to end due to the network cancelling it. He discussed feelings of shock, anger, frustration, and sadness. I have encountered children diagnosed with AS share intense feelings of sadness and grief over the loss of a pet and who exhibit feelings of shock, anger, and disappointment at the realization of the finality of this relationship. An adolescent diagnosed with AS was referred to me for depression and shared his "great sadness" over the loss of childhood and the intensity of feelings related to "not being able to go back there." A grown man diagnosed with AS literally shook as he cried and let out a deep guttural moan such as

I have never heard as he grieved the loss of his dear mother; his hands and arms squeezing me with the strength of a python as the full force of grief gripped him.

So why is there a misconception among teachers, counselors, therapists, psychologists, psychiatrists, and other professionals who think that children and teens diagnosed with AS are just robots that do not experience grief or sadness in the face of a great loss? I am not sure, but I encounter many who believe this misconception. I like to tell people that the child or adolescent diagnosed with AS does feel grief, sadness, and that the child or adolescent is fully aware of the loss, but often these amazing individuals are on another timetable with their grief than neurotypical people. Marston and Clarke (1999) discuss how autistic individuals can be caught off guard by losses and because of being unable to fully articulate feelings or understand feelings, the individual binds themselves even more intensely to stereotyped behaviors in order to cope and gain a sense of control. The bottom line for helping and connecting with children and adolescents dealing with grief and loss is to throw out expectations, agendas, or a preconceived notion of how grief should be for the child or adolescent diagnosed with AS and simply "just be" and allow yourself to be invited into their space at that given time and be curious about what you will find there.

Because many children and adolescents diagnosed with AS struggle with communicating thoughts and emotions due to the challenges that mindblindness and alexithymia bring, there can be a great deal of assumption on the part of parents and caregivers that the child or adolescent must be "internalizing" their grief and call upon the therapist to "pop the pimple" so to speak to get the child or adolescent to bring out their grief. I agree with Crenshaw and Mordock (2005) regarding a strength-based approach and that it is dangerous to assume that a child or adolescent is "pathological" based on the situation or challenges that they have encountered, and that "pouncing on pathology" (p. 53) can actually make things worse. While the challenges of AS make it more difficult to ascertain what is going on inside one of these remarkable individuals, therapists must use caution to not make assumptions or see the child or adolescent as damaged or handicapped. I have observed that some individuals diagnosed with AS are much better at weathering the storms of life than are neurotypical individuals. Like one teen diagnosed with AS said after Michael Jackson's death, "I don't see what the big deal is. Ninety-nine percent of these hysterical people never met the man in the first place."

Grief and loss issues for children and adolescents diagnosed with AS are similar to those discussed in the section on divorce. The child or adolescent diagnosed with AS can experience a range of emotional, behavioral, and relational problems when dealing with grief and loss. Similarly, the characteristics that are necessary for the therapist to be effective and create an environment of safety and trust with this unique population are the same that have been discussed previously. Patience, empathy, curiosity, imagination, a sense of humor, and a commitment to simply be present in order to understand are all part of effective grief and loss work with children and adolescents diagnosed with AS. A solid foundation of training and awareness of the issues of grief and loss is necessary as well, in addition to a commitment to helping family members, parents and caregivers understand their role in supporting the child or adolescent diagnosed with AS. In an effort to avoid being redundant, I have structured this section with play therapy approaches and techniques that I have found useful when working with children and adolescents diagnosed with AS experiencing grief and loss and provided case studies to help illustrate the technique.

Sand Play with Children and Adolescents Experiencing Grief or Loss

Sand play represents one of the most powerful healing approaches for children and adolescents who are experiencing grief and loss. This is due to the child or adolescent being able to play out and construct themes related to their internal processes regardless of verbal ability or emotional awareness. Due to these dynamics, sand play can be a valuable place of healing and exploration for the child or adolescent diagnosed with AS. When working with a child or adolescent diagnosed with AS who is experiencing grief and loss, it is important for the therapist to remember that the generalized atmosphere that the child or adolescent creates is key in understanding the material their individualized creation is communicating. Webber and Mascari (2008) discuss the following environmental considerations for themes of grief and loss in sand play:

1. Empty world symbolizing sadness and depression
2. Unpeopled world symbolizing pain or abuse
3. Fenced world or closed world symbolizing compartmentalized or protected issues
4. Rigid or schematic world or world of rows symbolizing control or hiding abuse
5. Disorganized world, incoherent world, or chaotic world symbolizing chaos
6. Aggressive world, with no humans except soldiers, symbolizing violence, anger.

The Case of Daniel: Saying Goodbye to Mom

Daniel was a twelve-year-old young man diagnosed with AS whose mother had died six months prior to entering therapy. His father brought him to counseling at the urging of school professionals who had noticed significant academic and social changes in Daniel, and the school counselor believed that it was partly due to grief and loss issues that he was dealing with. Daniel was not initially drawn to the sand box, and his case represents a scenario in which I prompted him to begin sand play by having him watch me play in the sand and inviting him to join me. Soon after, however, he took to the sand play and began to move the sand around and create lines and drawings in the sand. He did not put figures or structures in the sand, and he preferred the sand to be wet because "it was easier to draw in" and he would use a pencil or stick to make clean smooth lines. In our third session together he smoothed the sand with extra care creating a landscape that was clean and fresh and evenly balanced. He then picked up a thin plastic stick from an old "Pick-up Sticks" game and drew two flowers on either side of the sandbox and then in big letters wrote "Mom" in the center between the flowers. "My mom liked flowers" he said quietly. "I see" I responded. He then drew a house at the bottom of the sandbox with a dog, and three figures standing under a tree all holding hands. I have been trained to not talk during the sand play creation as Webber and Mascari (2008) suggest, however, with children and adolescents diagnosed with AS I do use some acknowledgement related to behavioral tracking to let them know that I am present and to give them the opportunity to expand on thoughts or emotions based on my observation of what is being created. In this case, however, I said nothing after the drawing of the family together as I believe that it spoke for itself and I am careful as I do not want to direct the child or adolescent toward a certain theme yet at times with children or adolescents diagnosed with AS some prompting may be necessary. I suggest that the therapist treat each case individually based on the unique characteristic of each child or adolescent and be prepared to modify a play therapy technique because of the uniqueness that AS brings to each individual that the therapist will encounter.

Over the next few sessions, it was as if Daniel was telling a story through the pictures he was drawing in the sandbox. There were drawings of him as a baby, early school experiences, and driving in the car with mom and dad. He then would smooth the sand and draw himself playing with mom watching in the background, as well as holidays and birthday parties. Themes soon began to emerge in the drawings related to things that mom liked such as flowers, jewelry, and books. If I could not make out what the drawing was, I would ask and Daniel would tell me. He spoke very little during the drawing sessions and I just simply sat on the floor with him and watched, feeling intrigued and honored to be a witness during this process. He then began to draw pictures with mom being in bed and in the hospital, and then drawings were drawn with intensity, with the stick being pushed deep into the sand and at times the lines had jagged edges and flecks of sand would fly out of the sandbox. His breathing became audible as he drew, his nostrils flaring with each exhale. I chose to not speak during this sequence, as I could clearly see that he was drawing out his mother's final months and days. I was so moved during these miraculous moments with this young man as my own mother had passed a year and a half prior, and I choked back tears trying very hard to not make a sound. I relaxed my core muscles in my stomach as I had learned in my trauma training and the tension released from my body. I was terrified that my reaction would startle him and disrupt this process, much like when a human encounters a rare animal in the wild at close range and is afraid to even breathe because the slightest startle or movement will end the encounter. My reaction quickly passed and I again focused fully on his process, and felt grateful that he did not look up during this brief section of time.

He then smoothed the sand completely and carefully, and took the stick and gently drew a tombstone with his mother's full name and flowers all around, including little sprigs of grass around the stone. He spent a great deal of time etching around the stone and his labored breathing was gone, a peaceful look was on his face. He said, "I know my mom is gone, but I know that she is still here." "Yes," I said, "It's like that, the person is not where we can see them but we know they are a part of us." He smiled and looked at the sandbox. "Do you erase my stuff after I leave?" he asked. "Yes" I said, "But only after you leave." He then told me he wanted to "get the sand smoothed out for the next kid" and I told him that was fine but I asked if he wanted me to take a picture of the grave marker he had drawn. He said "No" and explained that he could go to the gravesite and see it any time he wanted. He then spent a few minutes smoothing the sand and organizing the toys next to the sandbox. When he returned for the next session, he drew in the sand only briefly and the pictures had nothing to do with his mother. He then wanted to play a video game with me. In the sessions leading up to termination, he never again returned to the sandbox. His school performance improved and his father noticed Daniel was "his old self" at home and around the family.

Video Games and Grief and Loss

I have demonstrated the usefulness of computer and video games as a play-therapy tool with children suffering from emotional disturbances (Hull, 2009) as well as in previous sections of this book with children and adolescents diagnosed with AS. I agree with Attwood (2008) and LeGoff (2004) that utilizing the stereotyped interest of the child or adolescent can be a pathway for the therapist to make a connection with the young person and help the healing process begin. Many children and adolescents diagnosed with AS enjoy computer and video games and I often use this medium of play in therapy with grieving children and adolescents. Most computer and video games have themes of death in them; for instance, Mario "dies" when a Goomba or Bowser jumps on top of him. Other games have characters "dying" when the character falls off a cliff or smashes a car. The difference is that in the game one can easily "respawn" with a click of a button or start the level over. Losses in real life are final; the re-start button is nowhere to be found.

I worked with an eleven-year-old boy diagnosed with AS who was grieving the loss of his father, a man who had never been a part of his life but a man who this young boy yearned for nonetheless. As the boy was approaching pre-adolescence, his desire to know his father had increased and caused so much emotional disturbance that it prompted his mother to enter him in therapy and it was a theme of our work together. The boy liked video games and he especially liked games that had superheroes in them. He told me that he liked superhero characters because "they don't have dads either, but they are powerful." He shared with me that he found that most superheroes were either abandoned by their fathers ("just like me") or that their fathers were dead ("maybe my dad is dead"). As we played the game together, he would choose a different character to be and we would talk about the different "powers" of the characters. I used the character's strength as a metaphor for his abilities and talents, as well as the power to make wise choices. I also helped him see that many of the character's abilities did not come from their fathers, just like his abilities and talents were not nurtured by his father, but they were there nonetheless. Playing the games helped lead into an exploration of the feelings of missing his father and why those feelings were unpleasant for him, and allowed him a safe place for grief. He was able to talk about the feelings and come to understand them but also was able to gain strength from knowing that he, just like the superheroes he idolized, had many special gifts and talents. While he wished his father was in his life, over time in the therapy sessions he was able to accept that he was not in his life and to grieve that fact. His emotional problems subsided at home and at school after about twelve sessions of play therapy, and I continued to see him for about one year.

Music

Music can be effective as a part of therapy (Crenshaw and Mordock, 2005) and music has been explored as a therapy approach with children on the autism spectrum (Seville, 2007). I utilize music with adolescents and children on a regular basis. This may be through allowing a child to make up a song on an electric keyboard or play a harmonica, or have an adolescent bring in CD's that are special to them or look up music videos on the internet to gain a perspective of what inspires the young person. I have found that music can be useful in play therapy with children and adolescents diagnosed with AS, especially during times of grief and loss. One technique that I utilize is to have the child or adolescent make up a song on the keyboard and to use the various sounds that the keyboard is able to produce to freely create sounds—an experiment with sound. Some children and adolescents diagnosed with AS do not like the "din" that comes from unstructured musical exploration, so I show them some simple chords and teach how music is mathematical and able to be organized in synchronous, soothing sounds. The song becomes a way to identify with the emotions that the young person is feeling as well as to provide a marker for the grief experience.

Another technique that can be helpful in the grief process is to allow the young person diagnosed with AS to expose the therapist to the music that is meaningful to them. I worked with a young person about fourteen years old who was having difficulty expressing emotions regarding a significant loss he had experienced. I discovered that this young person liked music and listened to a unique form of heavy metal music. Like many of the young people diagnosed with AS who stumble upon unique and interesting "outside the box" interests, he had found a completely unique form of music called "Icelandic Metal." To his surprise, I grabbed my computer and we began to watch videos of his favorite groups and examine the lyrics. Through this process, the music opened up a pathway to deeper connection with his feelings and helped him give words to some of the pain he was feeling. One of the songs talked about choices and accepting what life brings and finding strength to carry on. I used the game of chess to help illustrate this, and we listened to the songs while we played. Had he not shared the music that he loved with me and had I not brought it into the therapy process, I doubt that I could have tapped into the emotions that he eventually ended up sharing because of the music.

Family Play and Grief and Loss

I have discussed previously the importance of involving parents and caregivers in the play-therapy process with children and adolescents diagnosed with AS. I believe that parents and caregivers play an important role in the grief process of their child or adolescent diagnosed with AS. Many parents and caregivers can be baffled by their child or adolescent diagnosed with AS because of the difficulties that mindblindness and alexithymia bring. For the child or adolescent and their family members experiencing grief and loss, parents, caregivers, and other family members can feel especially ill-equipped to meet the emotional needs and connect to the young person in a meaningful way during this difficult time. The process of play therapy that includes parents and caregivers can provide the reassurance of stability of relationship as well as improving understanding and connection between the young person diagnosed with AS and the parent or caregiver.

The *Play That Builds Connection* technique is useful during the grief and loss process to help the child or adolescent diagnosed with AS and the parent or caregiver build a stronger bond and improve communication and understanding. While the time of grief and loss can be a stressful time for the family and the child or adolescent, it can also present as an opportunity for deeper connection and improved relationship. The power of play provides a pathway for the parent or caregiver to get to a deeper level of understanding with the child or adolescent diagnosed with AS and provides both the child or adolescent and the parent or caregiver with the potential to heal through the deeper level of connection that play provides. By providing the parent or caregiver with the opportunity to engage in play and to learn techniques to utilize with the child or adolescent outside of the therapy office, the relationship between the two is strengthened and the potential for healing is increased.

Epilogue

Completing this work has been a great honor for me. I wish to thank all of the parents and caregivers, families, children, adolescents, and adults that have come my way over the years and who have introduced me to this fascinating world of Asperger's syndrome. I work very hard to help others see this world as it has been shown to me, and yet, because I am a neurotypical, it is as if I see this world only through a misty glass. During the writing of this work, I have found some great websites created by individuals diagnosed with AS and who candidly write on all sorts of topics, including past therapy experiences. As a therapist, I think it is important for us to be "out there" and listen to what these folks are saying and to be mindful of this as we conduct our therapy sessions. www.experienceproject.com/stories.php (keyword Asperger's Syndrome), http://life-with-Asperger's.blogspot.com, and www.wrongplanet .net are two examples of how we as therapists can get a better picture of the struggles of individuals who are trying to fit into a world that often does not make room for them. I recently came across a wonderful website called Asperger's Syndrome New Zealand (of, by, and for Kiwi Aspies!) and met a wonderful man named John Greally who, as an Aspie himself, works tirelessly to advocate for people like himself. He wrote a wonderful letter as a grown man to his parents, as he thought about how he felt as a child and what he wished he could have told them. I have received permission by John to reprint it here and I want to share it with you as I believe it says so wonderfully what I try and help parents and caregivers understand and feel from their children and adolescents, and to help children and adolescents communicate to their parents.

Kevin B. Hull
April 24, 2011

Johnny's Letter

Dear Mum and Dad,

I actually deeply, authentically, and completely LOVE you Mum and Dad. Really.

Knock, knock? Who's there? ME! There really IS someone home here Mum and Dad.

And I'll let you into my world—slowly—gently—quietly . . . but you just gotta remember that bit about "*when in Rome*" . . .

Occasionally I see that water trickle from your eyes, that sigh-breath thing you do, the slumped head-in-hands bit—that's you suspecting that because of my rather scarce emotional displays you're having doubts about my love. Don't doubt. You see, I don't do that sort of emotional display easily. Hugs often hurt. Kisses—yuck. Love is a decision, not mushy stuff for me . . . and I've long decided for YOU. Both of you. Guess what? You're my world too.

Still, sometimes I detect that *you know I love you,* but even then don't expect me to say it out loud, that would be a 'horribly inefficient duplication' of feelings . . . and a painful intense emotional interrupt to my functioning. An interruption to my need to manage internal temperatures, my anxieties, the coursing of powerful and even overwhelming feelings. Saying it out loud is a disabling brain activity. IQ-lowering stuff.

Yet, who do I talk to, stand with, go to, trust, show things to, think aloud to, sit with, cry in front of? No more misinterpretations, please: I am constantly saying "I love you, I love you, **I love YOU**"—that's all!

I know I seldom seem to listen *in the moment.* I know, but I do listen very very carefully, *even then.* That's why I know so much. (Sometimes too much).

145

Draw me a picture—I will photograph it and etch it deeply in white brain cells. Make me a book—I will chant it inside till known off-by-heart. I drink deeply from the well of who you are. I am after all a Repository of Information and Abider of Rules. Especially yours . . . and I really hear you in a way that, perhaps, no other can.

Don't be fooled by the merchants of glibness, money-makers, snake-oil merchants . . . for some are nothing short of purveyors of death . . . you see, I am <u>NOT</u> my behaviour. Never have been. That's just the stained and ripped book cover (*someone else did it—not me*). You see I have this long story inside me and it sort of encompasses my feelings and thoughts. All that has ever happened to me, all of the indescribable parts of me no one can see merely by "observing my behaviour," how and why I soar and plummet wildly, my thirst for justice and a sense of well-being, the euphoria I feel observing tiny rain drops on velour furred roses—and equally—spotting three ghastly matching weeds stood at attention in a neat row . . . everything, yes, everything. I do not want "how it all comes out" to define our relationship. I am much much more than that. You AND me both, eh!

I am not an alien, but you can help me to avoid being *alienated.* First by acknowledging you are weird to me too. Weird as. Except maybe Dad sometimes? Or maybe it's Mum whose strange at times? My genetic composition didn't come from outta nowhere y'know. You are even different from others of your own kind! Can we celebrate every single one of those differences together? Let's get out the crystal glasses and decanter kept in the special cupboard (the one I used to be fascinated with) . . . and drink merrily to that today!

While we're on that point about you being extra weird Dad, Mum, can one of you or both consider getting a diagnosis and publishing it in the newspaper for all to see? Esteem isn't built on back-patting and soothing affirmations alone. Sometimes we just gotta nail our colours to a very public mast. Sometimes we all gotta.

And if you don't get a diagnosis Dad or Mum, OK, but please leave me to "know" Autism. Do not claim to "know" it like I know it. Your job is to help me. To feel with me and all that stuff, but not to replace me—heh, not even on the local branch of my own autism organization!

You sometimes seriously underestimate the challenges I face most minutes of the day. Challenges created by my associated comorbids. Sometimes you are blinded by my abilities and forget my conditions' inherent complexities and all the apparent contradictions and paradoxes in Autism and Asperger's. You sometimes overlook my skill at surmounting these 'wicked' challenges, because of my resilience, my strategising and my ability to focus. Keep the balance guys. Please don't trip.

I learnt to spell words to show I am not retarded. Big words like "incontestable proof" and "paradoxical contradiction" and little words like "shove it" too. I know so much more than is seen in 'regular' communication. Communication I find so difficult to use. Communication that never seems enough to portray the 'meanings' I want to express—the exactnesses, the sensory connections, the whole of what I feel so outrageously inside.

Sometimes I need a rest from Asperger's Syndrome and Autism. Know what I mean? When I turn 18 and drink a little too much, I'm also gonna wanna be mainly legless for a while. OK? I want the dignity that comes from making similar mistakes to others. So, ah, let go appropriately. But don't let me stay in denial or always hide behind the non-appearance of my condition to satisfy some peer manipulation or any fears—I have some nailing up of colours to do also . . . eventually.

If you are going to help me do something, please make damned sure that your intention is that I'm gonna do it all my self later on. I embrace autonomy and independence . . . about as much as you let me . . . once my inertia is overcome. Sink or swim as an adult . . . it's up to you. Just like it is for every other child in the world too I guess.

Do not pay too much attention to any 'Triad of Impairments'—they are as valuable as zookeeper observations about monkeys at a tea party, well, to me anyway. Asperger's is much more about perspectives, preferences, porous timekeeping, profound focus, party foods, and being practically beaten up everyday by bullies. Really.

Asperger's is about processing information in different parts of the brain than 'typical' people and 'feeling' every sensory sensation. It's about 'seeing' the beauty found in all the details my brain doesn't get to filter out. The experts say I'm 'in my own world' but without all the brain filters removing so called 'unnecessary information,' I'm actually left *more* in the world. It's the 'normal' social-based world construction that I find difficult to be in.

This Autistic spectrum is so much bigger than it looks from the outside. I experience so many things which the 'experts' can't define and don't quite have words for . . . yet. It's a realm of diversity caused by a mind and body wired in a profoundly different way. In ways that dictate my behaviour and leave me suffering at the hands of others not prepared to understand—other people unprepared to get to know who I am on the inside and who *hurt* me. Really.

Hullo. Mum, Dad, what are you doing to stop Autism and Asperger's from remaining one of the least recognised, least diagnosed, least accommodated and least supported disabilities of the modern era? Despite these things, it *is* also one of the largest and most disabling conditions . . . worldwide. Mum, Dad, could you help the world to know this, please? I want a world to be a part of. I want my community. I want my culture. I want them to thrive. I want acceptance for myself and those of my kind.

If I am like a goldfish on the telephone table, flapping and gasping, do not treat my gasps as tardive dyskinesia—with medication. Do not anaesthetize my tail, eh . . . put me back in my goldfish bowl—I was never meant to be a fish out of water!

I am here the way I am here because God 'saw the need.' Now what's that, eh? Let's find out together. This is gonna be fun.

Don't grieve for me anymore. Or for yourself and all you're gonna miss out on because of how I am. If ya gotta grieve, cry for a world that doesn't understand me. Grieve for everything other people will miss out on by not getting to know me. Better still, join me in this adventure free of grief . . . it *will* be fun.

> I have decided for you,
> and that is all my love,
> (till I meet my other half perhaps,
> by such time my heart will have grown,
> and there never need be any loss felt by all,
>   . . . on the contrary),

Your son,
Johnny

Bibliography

Activision. 2005. Call of Duty 2. Santa Monica: Activision Inc.

Ackerman, S. J., and Hilsenroth, M. J. 2003. "A Review of Therapist Characteristics and Techniques Positively Impacting the Therapeutic Alliance." *Clinical Psychology Review* 23: 1–33.

Ahrons, C. 2007. "No Easy Answers: Why the Popular View of Divorce Is Wrong." *Shifting the Center: Understanding Contemporary Families*, 3rd ed., 523–34. New York, NY: McGraw-Hill.

Ahrons, C. R. 2007. "Family Ties after Divorce: Long-Term Implications for Children." *Family Process,* 46(1), 53–65. doi:10.1111/j.1545–5300.2006.00191.x.

Ahrons, C., and Marquardt, E. 2010. "Does Divorce Have Positive Long-Term Effects for the Children Involved?" In B. Slife, B. Slife (Eds.), *Clashing Views on Psychological Issues*, 16th ed., 134–54. New York, NY: McGraw-Hill.

American Psychiatric Association. 2000. *Diagnostic and Statistical Manual of Mental Disorders*, 4th ed., text revision. Washington, DC, American Psychiatric Association.

Attwood T. 1998. *Asperger's Syndrome: A Guide for Parents and Professionals.* London, UK: Jessica Kingsley Publishers.

Attwood, T. 2007. *The Complete Guide to Asperger's Syndrome.* London, UK: Jessica Kingsley Publishers.

Axline, V. M. 1964. *Dibs: in Search of Self: Personality Development in Play Therapy.* Boston, MA: Houghton Mifflin.

Barnhill, G. P. 2001. "Social Attributions and Depression in Adolescents with Asperger Syndrome." *Focus on Autism and Other Developmental Disabilities* 16, no. 1: 46–53.

Barnhill, G. P., and Myles, B. 2001. "Attributional Style and Depression in Adolescents with Asperger Syndrome." *Journal of Positive Behavior Interventions,* 3(3), 175–82. doi:10.1177/109830070100300305.

149

Barnhill, G. P. 2004. "Asperger Syndrome: A Guide for Secondary School Principals." *Principal Leadership Magazine* 5(3). Retrieved from http://www.nasponline.org/resources/principals/nassp_asperger.aspx.

Baron-Cohen, S. 1995. *Mindblindness: An essay on autism and theory of mind.* Cambridge, MA: The MIT Press.

Baron-Cohen, S. 2002. "The Extreme Male Brain Theory of Autism." *Trends in Cognitive Sciences,* 6(6), 248–254. doi:10.1016/S1364–6613(02)01904–6.

Baron-Cohen, S. 2009. "The Short Life of a Diagnosis." Retrieved from www.nytimes.com/2009/11/10/opinion/10baron-cohen.html?_r=1&ref=opinion.

Bradway, K., and McCoard, B. 1997. *Sandplay: Silent Psyche of the Soul.* New York, NY: Routledge/Taylor & Francis Group.

Bromfield, R. 1989. "Psychodynamic Play Therapy with a High-Functioning Autistic Child." *Psychoanalytic Psychology,* 6(4), 439–53. Doi:10.1037/0736–9735.6.4.439.

Bromfield, R. 2010. *Doing Therapy with Children and Adolescents with Asperger Syndrome.* Hoboken, NJ: John Wiley & Sons Inc.

Carter, S. 2009. "Bullying of Students with Asperger Syndrome." *Issues in Comprehensive Pediatric Nursing,* 32(3), 145–154. doi:10.1080/01460860903062782.

Crenshaw, D., and Mordock, J. 2005. *Understanding and Treating the Aggression of Children: Fawns in Gorilla Suits.* Lanham, MD: Jason Aronson.

Crenshaw, D. A., and Hardy, K. V. 2007. "The Crucial Role of Empathy in Breaking the Silence of Traumatized Children in Play Therapy." *International Journal of Play Therapy,* 16(2), 160–75. doi:10.1037/1555–6824.16.2.160.

Dubowski, J., and Evans, K. 2001. *Art Therapy with Children on the Autistic Spectrum: Beyond Words.* London, UK: Jessica Kingsley Publishers.

Edgette, J. 2006. *Adolescent Therapy That Really Works: Helping Kids Who Never Asked for Help in the First Place.* New York, NY: W W Norton & Co.

Electronic Arts. 2003. The Sims. [DISC]. PlayStation2. London: Electronic Arts Inc.

Epp, K. 2008. "Outcome-Based Evaluation of a Social Skills Program Using Art Therapy and Group Therapy for Children on the Autism Spectrum." *Children & Schools,* 30(1), 27–36.

Fanning, E. and Brighton, C. 2007. "The Sims in Therapy: an Examination of Feasibility and Potential of the Use of Game-Based Learning in Clinical Practice." In B. K. Weiderhold, G. Riva, S. Bouchard (Eds.), *Annual Review of Cybertherapy and Telemedicine: Advanced Technologies in the Behavioral, Social, and Neurosciences,* 5, 1–11. ISSN: 1554–8716.

Fitzgerald, M., and Bellgrove, M. A. 2006. "The Overlap between Alexithymia and Asperger's Syndrome." *Journal of Autism and Developmental Disorders,* 36(4), 573–576. doi:10.1007/s10803–006–0096-z.

Firth, U. 1991. *Autism and Asperger Syndrome.* Cambridge, UK: Cambridge University Press.

Gallo-Lopez, L., and Schaefer, C. (Eds.). 2005. *Play Therapy with Adolescents.* Lanham, MD: Jason Aronson.

Gardner, R. A. 1973. The Talking, Feeling, Doing Game. Creskill, NJ: Creative Therapeutics.

Gellar, L. 2005. "Emotional Regulation and Autism Spectrum Disorders." *Autism Spectrum Quarterly*. (Summer, 2005). Retrieved from www.aspfi.org/documents/gellerasq.pdf.

Ghaziuddin, M., Ghaziuddin, N., and Greden, J. 2002. "Depression in Persons with Autism: Implications for Research and Clinical Care." *Journal of Autism and Developmental Disorders*, 32(4), 299–306. doi:10.1023/A:1016330802348.

Gillberg, C. 1991. "Clinical and Neurobiological Aspects of Asperger's Syndrome in Six Families Studied." In *Autism and Asperger's Syndrome* (ed. U. Frith), 122–46. Cambridge, UK: Cambridge University Press.

Greenspan, S. I., and Wieder, S. 2007. "The Developmental Individual-Difference, Relationship-Based (DIR/Floortime) Model Approach to Autism Spectrum Disorders." In E. Hollander, E. Anagnostou, E. Hollander, E. Anagnostou (Eds.), *Clinical Manual for the Treatment of Autism*, 179–209. Arlington, VA: American Psychiatric Publishing, Inc.

Hall, T. M., Kaduson, H., and Schaefer, C. E. 2002. "Fifteen Effective Play Therapy Techniques." *Professional Psychology: Research and Practice*, 33(6), 515–22. doi:10.1037/0735–7028.33.6.515.

Hartley, S. L., Barker, E. T., Seltzer, M., Floyd, F., Greenberg, J., Orsmond, G., and Bolt, D. (2010). "The Relative Risk and Timing of Divorce in Families of Children with an Autism Spectrum Disorder." *Journal of Family Psychology*, 24(4), 449–57. doi:10.1037/a0019847.

Hénault, I., and Attwood, T. 2005. *Asperger's Syndrome and Sexuality: From Adolescence through Adulthood*. London, UK: Jessica Kingsley Publishers.

Hull, K. 2009. "Computer/Video Games as a Play Therapy Tool in Reducing Emotional Disturbances in Children." *Dissertation Abstracts International*, 70.

Jackson, L. 2002. *Freaks, Geeks and Asperger Syndrome: A User Guide to Adolescence*. London, UK: Jessica Kingsley Publishers.

Jacobsen, P. 2004. "A Brief Overview of the Principles of Psychotherapy with Asperger's Syndrome." *Clinical Child Psychology and Psychiatry*, 9(4), 567–78. doi:10.1177/1359104504046160.

Jagex. 2002. RuneScape. Cambridge, UK: Jagex Inc.

Kerr, C., Hoshino, J., Sutherland, J., Parashak, S., and McCarley, L. 2008. *Family Art Therapy: Foundations of Theory and Practice*. New York, NY: Routledge/Taylor & Francis Group.

Koocher, G. P., and D'Angelo, E. J. 1992. "Evolution of Practice in Child Psychology." In D. K. Freedheim, H. J. Freudenberger, J. W. Kessler, S. B. Messer, and D. R. Peterson (Eds.), *History of Psychotherapy: A Century of Change* 457–492. Washington DC: American Psychological Association.

Laurent, A. C., and Rubin, E. 2004. "Challenges in Emotional Regulation in Asperger Syndrome and High-Functioning Autism." *Topics in Language Disorders*, 24(4), 286–97.

Leblanc, M., and Ritchie, M. 2001. "A Meta-Analysis of Play Therapy Outcomes." *Counselling Psychology Quarterly*, 14(2), 149–163.

LeGoff, D. B. 2004. "Use of LEGO© as a Therapeutic Medium for Improving Social Competence." *Journal of Autism and Developmental Disorders*, 34(5), 557–71. doi:10.1007/s10803–004–2550–0.

Lesinskiene, S. 2002. "Children with Asperger Syndrome: Specific Aspects of Their Drawings." *International Journal of Circumpolar Health* 2002; 61 Suppl 2:90–6.

Lozzi-Toscano, B. 2004. "The 'Dance' of Communication: Counseling Families and Children with Asperger's Syndrome." *The Family Journal*, 12(1), 53–57. doi:10.1177/1066480703258805.

Lu, L., Peterson, F., LaCroix, L., and Rousseau, C. 2010. "Stimulating Creative Play in Children with Autism Through Sand Play." *The Arts in Psychotherapy*, 37(1), 56–64.

Marston, G. M., and Clarke, D. J. 1999. "Making Contact—Bereavement and Asperger's Syndrome." *Irish Journal of Psychological Medicine*, 16(1), 29–31.

Milgrom, C. 2005. "An Introduction to Play Therapy with Adolescents." In L. Gallo-Lopez, C. E. Schaefer, L. Gallo-Lopez, C. E. Schaefer (Eds.), *Play Therapy With Adolescents* 3–17. Lanham, MD: Jason Aronson.

"MTV and the Associated Press Release Landmark Study of Young People and Happiness," Thinkmtv—Research, August 20, 2007, available from www.mtv.com/thinkmtv/research; Internet.

Munro, J. 2010. "An Integrated Model of Psychotherapy for Teens and Adults with Asperger Syndrome." *Journal of Systemic Therapies*, 29(3), 82–96. doi:10.1521/jsyt.2010.29.3.82.

Neufeld, D., and Wolfberg, P. 2010. "From Novice to Expert: Guiding Children on the Autism Spectrum in Integrated Play Groups." In C. E. Schaefer, C. E. Schaefer (Eds.), *Play Therapy for Preschool Children*, 277–299. Washington, DC: American Psychological Association. doi:10.1037/12060–013.

Norton, C. C., and Norton, B. E. 1997. *Reaching Children through Play Therapy: An Experiential Approach*. Denver, CO: Pendleton Clay Publishers.

Rao, P. A., Beidel, D. C., and Murray, M. J. 2008. "Social Skills Interventions for Children with Asperger's Syndrome or High-Functioning Autism: A Review and Recommendations." *Journal of Autism and Developmental Disorders*, 38(2), 353–61. doi:10.1007/s10803–007–0402–4.

Robison, J. E. 2007. "Look Me in the Eye: My Life With Asperger's." New York, NY: Three Rivers Press.

Rothschild, B. 2000. *The Body Remembers: The Psychophysiology of Trauma and Trauma Treatment*. New York, NY: W W Norton & Co.

Russell, E., and Sofronoff, K. 2005. "Anxiety and Social Worries in Children with Asperger Syndrome." *Australian and New Zealand Journal of Psychiatry*, 39(7), 633–638. doi:10.1111/j.1440–1614.2005.01637.x.

Saunders, S. M. 2001. Pretreatment Correlates of the Therapeutic Bond. *Journal of Clinical Psychology*, 57: 1339–52.

Schaefer, C. E. 2001. "Prescriptive Play Therapy." *International Journal of Play Therapy,* 10(2), 57–73. doi:10.1037/h0089480.

Schreiber, C. 2011. "Social Skills Interventions for Children with High-Functioning Autism Spectrum Disorders." *Journal of Positive Behavior Interventions,* 13(1), 49–62. doi:10.1177/1098300709359027.

Seville, R. 2007. "Music Therapy and Autistic Spectrum Disorder." In T. Watson, T. Watson (Eds.), *Music Therapy with Adults with Learning Disabilities,* 33–46. New York, NY: Routledge/Taylor & Francis Group.

Shaffer, G., and Lazarus, R. 1952. *Special Psychotherapies. Fundamental Concepts in Clinical Psychology,* 386–408. New York, NY: McGraw-Hill Book Company.

Shtayermman, O. 2008. "Suicidal Ideation and Comorbid Disorders in Adolescents and Young Adults Diagnosed with Asperger's Syndrome: A Population at Risk." *Journal of Human Behavior in the Social Environment,* 18(3), 301–28. doi:10.1080/10911350802427548.

Skigen, D. 2008. "Taking the Sand Tray High Tech: Using the Sims as a Therapeutic Tool in the Treatment of Adolescents." In L. C. Rubin, L. C. Rubin (Eds.), *Popular Culture in Counseling, Psychotherapy, and Play-Based Interventions,* 165–79. New York, NY: Springer Publishing Co.

Tantam, D. 1991. "Asperger Syndrome in Adulthood." In U. Frith (Ed.), *Autism and Asperger Syndrome,* 147–83. Cambridge, UK: Cambridge University Press.

Van Velsor, P. 2004. "Revisiting Basic Counseling Skills with Children." *Journal of Counseling & Development,* 82(3), 313–18.

VanFleet, R. 1994. "Filial Therapy for Adoptive Children and Parents." In K. J. O'Connor, C. E. Schaefer, K. J. O'Connor, C. E. Schaefer (Eds.), *Handbook of Play Therapy, Vol. 2: Advances and Innovations,* 371–85. Oxford, UK: John Wiley & Sons.

Volkmar, F. R., Klin, A., Siegal, B., Szatmari, P., Lord, C., and Campbell, M. 1994. "Field Trial for Autistic Disorder in DSM IV." *American Journal of Psychiatry,* 151, 1361–67.

Webber, J., and Mascari, J. B. 2008. *Sand Play Therapy and the Healing Process in Trauma and Grief Counseling.* Retrieved from counselingoutfitters.com/vistas/vistas08/Webber.htm.

Weber, K. 2008. "Asperger's Syndrome: From Hiding to Thriving." *Nurse Practitioner:* July 2008 33(7), 14–21. doi: 10.1097/01.NPR.0000325974.78130.72.

Welkowitz, L. A., and Baker, L. J. 2005. "Supporting College Students with Asperger's Syndrome." In L. J. Baker, L. A. Welkowitz, L. J. Baker, L. A. Welkowitz (Eds.), *Asperger's Syndrome: Intervening in Schools, Clinics, and Communities,* 173–87. Mahwah, NJ: Lawrence Erlbaum Associates Publishers.

Wing, L. 1981. "Asperger's Syndrome: A Clinical Account." *Psychological Medicine: A Journal of Research in Psychiatry and the Allied Sciences* 11, no. 1: 115–29.

Wing, L. 2005. "Reflections on Opening Pandora's Box." *Journal of Autism and Developmental Disorders,* 35, no. 2: 197–203.

Index

abundance mindset, 74
Activision, 86; *See also* Call of Duty
  Modern Warfare 2 (video game)
Adam (film), 11
Ahrons, C., 113, 127
alexithymia, 28, 36, 114, 135, 140
Allen, Ronald, ix
America's Most Wanted (TV show), 4,
  17
American Psychological Association,
  7–8
Anxiety. *See* fears
art. *See* play therapy with adolescents;
  play therapy with children
art therapy. *See* play therapy with
  adolescents; play therapy with
  children
Asperger, Hans, 7, 9, 11
Asperger's syndrome (AS), xii, 7, 143;
  challenges of, 3; diagnostic criteria
  of, 8–10; history of, 7–8; in modern
  culture, 11–12; in modern mental
  health and education, 11; symptoms
  expanded upon, 10
"Aspergians," 12
"Aspies," 12, 82, 143
Attwood T., x, 5, 26, 35, 58, 68, 8 3, 90,
  99, 138

autism, x, 4, 7–8, 15, 30, 32, 40, 44, 47,
  139, 146–147
Axline, V. M., 31, 37

Baker, L. J., 74
Barbie dolls, 71
Barker, E. T., 30
Barnhill, G. P., 63–64, 68, 70, 87
Baron–Cohen, S., x, 5, 7, 8, 15–16,
  28–29, 32, 64–65, 70
barriers: conversational, 13; relational,
  15; social, 15
Beanie Babies, 38–39
behavioral tracking, 4, 23–24, 37,
  121–122, 137
Beidel, D. C., 68
Bellgrove, M. A., 16, 28, 67
board games. *See* play therapy with
  adolescents; play therapy with
  children
Bolt, D., 30
Bradway, K., 124, 129
brain, 16–17, 23, 28, 36, 59–60, 70, 91,
  100, 105–106, 124, 145–147
Brighton, C., 106
Bromfield, R., x, 5, 32, 55, 60, 99
building self-worth. *See* play therapy
  with adolescents

bullying, 2, 11, 27–28, 42, 44, 64–68, 70–71, 73, 80, 89–94, 96, 98, 128
bullying and social rejection. *See* play therapy with adolescents
Buzz Lightyear, 102

Call of Duty Modern Warfare 2 (video game), 86
Campbell, M., 7
Carter, S., 28, 64
case studies: Brian, 51–53; Daniel, 137–138; Jason, 110–112; Roger, 1–3
challenges: of living with AS, 12
chess. *See* play therapy with adolescents; play therapy with children
Clarke, D. J., 135
communication: creating with adolescents, 59–62; play therapy with adolescents as the vehicle of, 80
computer and video games. *See* play therapy with adolescents
connection: creating with adolescents, 55–58
Crenshaw, D. A., ix, 21, 25–26, 31, 70, 135, 139

D'Angelo, E. J., 31
depression, 28–29, 63–64, 87–89, 110, 116, 118, 134, 136
divorce, 113–114; behavioral effects, 116–117; emotional effects, 114–116; parent and caregiver considerations, 118; play therapy for adolescents, 128–134; play therapy for children, 120–128; relational effects, 117–118; therapist considerations, 119–120
DSM IV-TR, 7–9
DSM V-TR, 7–8
Dubowski, J., 33

Edgette, J., 55
Electronic Arts, 91

emotional immaturity, 11, 68, 70–72, 79, 103, 114, 128–129
emotional regulation, 68–69, 103, 105, 114, 128, 131; *See also* play therapy with adolescents; themes with adolescents diagnosed with AS
empathy: deficits, 18; divorce and grief/ loss, 119, 128, 136; group therapy process, 102; in the therapy process, 6, 12, 22, 25–27; lack of, 10; modeling of by therapist, 60
encouragement, 12, 42, 76, 106, 108–109
Epp, K., 33, 40, 95, 101
Evans, K., 33

family stress, 29–30, 72, 74
family systems, xii, 49
Fanning, E., 106
fears: adolescents, 68, 86, 92, 107–108, 114; case study of Brian, 51–53; case study of Jason, 112; case study of Roger, 2; children, 26–27, 32–35, 37–38, 114, 125; Johnny's letter, 147; parents and family, 29, 48, 72, 74–75, 84
fight-or-flight, 28, 30, 70, 93, 104–105, 115, 124, 131
Fitzgerald, M., 16, 28, 67
Florida Baptist Children's Home, xi
Floyd, F., 30
Frith, Uta, 7

Gallo-Lopez, L., 79
The Game of LIFE, 49, 108
game play. *See* play therapy with adolescents; play therapy with children
games. *See* play therapy with adolescents; play therapy with children
Gardner, R. A., 101
Gellar, L., 69,
Ghaziuddin, M., 64
Ghaziuddin, N., 64

G I Joe, 81
Gillberg, C., 9, 93
give your therapist a good shove! *See*
  play therapy with adolescents
Grandin, Temple, 12
Greally, John, x, 143
Greden, J., 64
Greenberg, J., 30
Greenspan, S. I., 47
grief and loss, 134–141
group play. *See* play therapy with
  adolescents; play therapy with
  children

Hall, T. M., 151
Hardy, K. V., 25–26
Hartley, S. L., 30, 75
Hénault, I., 99
hope, 12, 74, 76–77, 84, 109
Hoshino, J., 50
Hull, K., 34, 45, 85, 138

The Incredible Hulk, 102
insight-oriented therapies: resistance
  to, 17
internalize, 67, 91, 96, 114, 123

Jackson, L., 63, 135
Jacobsen, P., 21
Jagex, 83, 87–88
Johnny's letter, 145
joint attention deficits, 16, 36, 71–72
"just be," 5, 22, 48, 111–112, 135

Kaduson, H., 151
Kerr, C., 50
Klein, Melanie, 31
Klin, A., 7
Koocher, G. P., 31

Lambert, Jack, xi
Landreth, Garry, 31
Laurent, A. C., 69
LaCroix, L., 31
Lazarus, R., 31

Leblanc, M., 31
Lego, 1, 3, 4, 24, 32–33, 38–41, 43, 48,
  51–52, 71, 127, 130
Lego Harry Potter (video game), 33, 41
Lego Indiana Jones (video game), 33,
  35, 41, 52–53, 124–125
Lego Star Wars (video game), 3, 33, 35,
  38–39, 41, 45, 124
LeGoff, D. B., x, 5, 31–32, 35, 40, 58,
  83, 138
Lesinskiene, S., 33–34
Lincoln Logs, 127, 130
Look Me in the Eye (book), 12, 14
Lord, C., 7
Lozzi-Toscano, B., 29, 46, 74
Lu, L., 31, 40, 44, 81, 120

Marquardt, E., 127
Marston, G. M., 135
Mascari, J. B., 136–137
McCarley, L., 50
McCoard, B., 124, 129
metaphor, 33, 35, 37–38, 44–46, 52, 58,
  61–62, 80, 84–88, 93, 102, 104, 112,
  126, 139
Milgrom, C., 81
mindblindness, 28, 36, 93, 135, 140
Mordock, J., 135, 139
motor clumsiness, 93
Mozart and the Whale (film), 11
MTV, 55
multi-tasking of therapist, 70
Munro, J., 3, 68, 76
Murray, M. J., 68
music in therapy, 139–140
Myles, B., 87

National Autistic Society, 11
Neufeld, D., 40, 101
neurotypical, 12–13, 15–16, 28–29, 36,
  48–49, 60–63, 66, 72, 75–77, 80, 97,
  108, 116–118, 130–131, 135, 143
neurotypical siblings, 48–49, 77
Nintendo NES, 92, 105; *See also* Super
  Mario Bros.; Mario Bros.

non-reactivity, 22, 53, 102, 130
Norton, B. E., ix, xii, 31, 38, 43–44, 79, 120
Norton, C. C., 31, 38, 43–44, 79, 120

obsessive compulsive disorder (OCD), 24, 27, 29, 34, 44, 50–51, 117
obsessive thinking, 16
online role-playing games (RPGS), 83
Orsmond, G., 30

Parashak, S., 50
patience: of the therapist, 6, 60–61, 84, 102, 119, 136
Peterson, F., 31
The Pez game. *See* play therapy with adolescents; play therapy with children
physical activities, *See* play therapy with adolescents
pillow boxing. *See* play therapy with adolescents
Pink Floyd, 22
Pittsburgh Steelers, xi
Play that Builds Connection: relating to the issue of divorce, grief and loss, 127, 132–133, 141; with children, 47–49
play therapy: non-directive, 31, 37, 123; directive, 31; *See also* play therapy with adolescents; play therapy with children
play therapy techniques, 119; *See also* play therapy with adolescents; play therapy with children
play therapy with adolescents: art, 88–89; building self-worth, 83–89; bullying and social rejection, 89–98; chess, 92–93; computer and video games, 83–88, 104–106; emotional regulation and emotional maturity, 103–106, 128; game play, 99–100; give your therapist a good shove!, 96–98; group play, 100–101;

improving social skills, 98–103; physical activities, 93–98; pillow boxing, 95–96; play therapy to help families of adolescents, 108–110; rational, 79–81; role-playing social situations, 103; sand play, 129–130; swordfights, 94–95; The Game of LIFE, 108; The PEZ game, 102; The Sims game, 106–107, 128–129; The Talking, Feeling, Doing game, 101–102; transitions of life, 106–108; video games, 90–92
play therapy with children: art, 33–34; building, 43; chess, 38; conquering fear, 32–36; get in their world!, 41–42; group play, 40–41; I am unique! technique, 42–43; increase self-worth, 41–46; Lego play, 32–33; puppets and stuffed animals, 32, 38–40; road maps and city streets, 36–38; sand play, 43–45; social skills and dealing with emotional difficulties, 36–41; video games, 34–36, 45–46
Pokemon, 10, 80
"pouncing on pathology," 135
puppet play. *See* play therapy with adolescents; play therapy with children

Rao, P. A., 68, 73
reflective listening, 4
rejection, 27–29, 42, 44, 64–66, 68, 76, 89, 94, 110, 112
respect, 57, 82–83, 88, 102
restricted interests, 16
road maps and city streets. *See* play therapy with children
role-playing, 52, 83, 96, 101–103
role-playing social situations. *See* play therapy with adolescents
Ritchie, M., 31
Robison, John Elder, 12
Rothschild, B., 28, 70

Rousseau, C., 31
Rubin, E., 69
RuneScape (computer game), 10, 83, 87, 88
Russell, E., 26–28

sand play: for increasing self-worth, 44; relating to divorce, 120–124; relating to grief/loss, 136; *See also* play therapy with children; play therapy with adolescents
Saunders, S. M., 21
scarcity mindset, 74
Schaefer, C., 31, 79
Shaffer, G., 31
Schreiber, C., 152
self-soothe, 130–132
Seltzer, M., 30
Seville, R., 139
Shrek, 102
Shtayermman, O., 64
Siegel, B., 7
silence, 22–23, 59–61, 111
The Sims Game (computer game), 106–107, 128–129
Skigen, D., 106
Sligh, Michael, ix
social interactions, 12, 71, 76, 80, 107
social rejection, 28, 42, 64–65, 68, 89, 94
social skills: case study of Jason, 112; deficits, 67–69; increasing in adolescents, 85–86, 91–92, 98–103; increasing in children, 36–41; modeling by family members, 47–48, 50; modeling by therapist, 32; relationship barriers, 16–17; use of Lego, 32–33
Sofronoff, K., 26–28
Sorry! (game), 49
Spiderman, 102
Star Wars (movie), 28, 39, 42, 44–45; clones, 35, 44
stereotyped interests, 35, 52, 58, 83, 117

stuffed animals. *See* play therapy with children
suicide, 63–64, 118
Super Mario Brothers (video games), 35, 41, 92, 139; Bowser, 139; Goomba, 139; Luigi, 92; Mario, 92
Sutherland, J., 50
swordfights. *See* play therapy with adolescents
sympathetic nervous system, 70, 89, 93, 104, 106, 124
Szatmari, P., 7

The Talking, Feeling, Doing game. *See* play therapy with adolescents
Tantam, D., 73
tantrums, 27–28, 51, 53, 70, 98, 106, 116, 124–125
Tetris (video game), 105, 131, 132
themes with adolescents diagnosed with AS: bullying and social rejection, 65–67; emotional regulation difficulties and emotional maturity, 68–72; family stress, 74–78; low self-worth, 63–65; social skills deficit, 67–68; transitions, 72–74
themes with children diagnosed with AS: family stress, 29–30; fear, 26–27; low self-worth, 28–29; social and relational difficulties, 27–28
therapeutic alliance, 21–22, 119; *See also* therapeutic alliance building techniques
therapeutic alliance building techniques: follow directions, 24; get comfortable with silence, 22–23; "just be," 22; let your imagination be part of the process, 25; use of behavioral tracking, 23–24
therapeutic relationship, 4, 16–17, 23, 35, 56, 62, 99, 119
toys and techniques to help parents/ caregivers/families: board games,

48–50; family art projects, 50; Play that Builds Connection, 47–48
Thinking in Pictures (film), 11
Thomas, John, ix
Tinker Toys, 41, 127
Toy Story (film), 102
transitions of life. *See* play therapy with adolescents
trust: and empathy, 26; building between therapist and child or adolescent, 4, 16, 21, 24, 41, 57, 79–80, 84, 99, 119, 133, 136; case of Brian, 52; case of Jason, 111; during divorce, 117, 120, 127; lack of, 5, 26; with parents and therapists, 58

UNO (card game), 49–50
unrealistic parent expectations, 18

VanFleet, R., 31, 47
Van Velsor, P., 23
video games, *See* play therapy with children; play therapy with adolescents
Volkmar, F. R., 7

Wahoo (game), 100, 109
Waters, Roger, 22
Webber, J., 136, 137
Weber, K., 7
Welkowitz, L. A., 74
Wieder, S., 47
Wii Sports (video games), 35
Wing, L., 7, 11, 63
Wolfberg, P., 101
World of Warcraft (video game), 10, 83

About the Author

Kevin B. Hull, Ph.D, LMHC, owns a private counseling practice in Lakeland, Florida where he has practiced for the past eleven years and specializes in using play therapy with children and adolescents diagnosed with Asperger's syndrome. Prior to working in private practice, he worked in numerous community mental health settings. He was an adjunct professor for Webster University's Masters of Counseling Lakeland Campus for eight years and is a professor for Liberty University Online Masters of Counseling program. He and his wife Wendy have four children, a Dachshund, Quaker parrot, Guinea pig, and many fish.